THE HUNT
FOR BIG STRIPERS

ZENO HROMIN

B.

880

lt - 4164

All inquiries should be addressed to

Zeno Hromin
P.O. BOX 10665
Westbury, NY 11590
Or visit our website at
www.zenohromin.com

IBSN 978-1-60702-761-4

Design and Layout: Stacey Kruk, SK Graphics, www.skgraphics.net
Illustrations: Tommy Corrigan
Cover Photo: David Ryng and Zeno Hromin
Cover Design: Alberto Knie

Other books by author

The Art of Surfcasting with Lures

For more information about this book please visit
www.zenohromin.com

DEDICATION

For Jennie,
My Best Catch

ACKNOWLEDGMENTS

Putting this book together has been an eye-opening experience. Not because of the work involved but because I have already benefited from reading the chapters written by some of the most successful surfcasters that ply the suds today. I have used their suggestions, strategies and techniques to catch bigger fish only a few days after reading their chapters. I strongly believe that you will experience similar results.

With that in mind, I have to express a great deal of appreciation to John Skinner, Steve McKenna, William "Doc" Muller, "Crazy" Alberto Knie, Jimmy D'Amico and Manny Moreno for helping me bring this project to fruition.

Special thanks goes to Howard Marshall, Jim Criscione and Richard Giovelli who helped out with some editing and my friends, Tommy Corrigan and Robert Maina who always pick up the phone when I call with questions, even when they know they shouldn't.

Appreciation also goes to Al Bentsen for his advice and guidance and also to Lenny Ferro who was seemingly always in the right place at the right time this season. Thankfully, I always had a camera on me to capture his triumphs.

My eternal gratitude goes to Ed Messina and the dynamic duo of Roger Martin and his wife Marie, who labored through my writing, trying to make some sense of it all.

I also want to express my sincerest appreciation to all of my friends who allowed me to use their pictures in this book. For that I will be eternally grateful. Thanks to Steve McKenna, Manny Moreno, John Skinner, William " Doc" Muller, "Crazy" Alberto Knie, Jimmy D'Amico, Tommy Corrigan, Dennis Wolf, Al Bentsen, Lenny Ferro, Patricia Hewlett, Peter Hewlett, Al Albano, Nick Colabro, Robert Maina, Pete Peresh, David Ryan, Terence Kirby, Ryan Smith, Louis DeRicco, John Marc Basile, James Sylvester, Josh Clogston, Mike Ludlow, Jim Faulkner, Joe Martins, John Rich, David Ryng, James Sylvester, Al Pellini and Mike Didyk.

— Zeno Hromin

ABOUT THE AUTHORS

ZENO HROMIN is a veteran surfcaster whose previous book *"The Art of Surfcasting with Lures"* has received rave reviews from surfcasters along the striper coast. Called a "surfcasting bible", this book has become the new reference guide for any surfcaster looking to improve his success when fishing with lures. He is a frequent contributor to northeast fishing publications in print and on the Internet and he is a frequent speaker at fishing shows in the Northeast. Zeno is a member of the New York State Outdoor Writers Association and the High Hill Striper Club of Long Island, New York.

JIMMY D'AMICO is the driving force behind the Hunter Surfcasting Gear Company. As a designer, tester, manufacturer and, most importantly, an end user, Jimmy's designs are often inspired by his own relentless pursuit of perfection. An extremely aggressive wetsuiter, Jimmy can often be found bobbing in the dark waters off Montauk Point looking for a rock he can cast from.

STEVE MCKENNA is one of today's most successful New England surfcasters. Although he lives in Rhode Island, Steve has traveled extensively in search of large fish. He is equality adept at pulling big stripers from the jagged rocks of Block Island as he is at dragging cows onto the sandy beaches of Cape Cod. In recent years, Steve's approach to rigging plastic baits, particularly Slug-go's, has revolutionized the way surfcasters fish with plastics. His success with large fish has resulted in the increased availability of many different types of eel alternatives on store shelves today. Steve has written for local and regional publications in New England and is a frequent speaker on the fishing show circuit.

JOHN SKINNER is the long-time surf fishing columnist of Nor'east Saltwater Magazine. He has written articles for many publications in the Northeast and is a frequent speaker at outdoor shows. His recent book *"A Season on the Edge"* has received rave reviews in the surf fishing community. John is considered to be one of the most successful big fish

hunters of the current generation. Quiet and unassuming, he prefers anonymity to fame. If you ever get lucky enough to fish alongside him, watch his every move.

MANNY MORENO is the type of angler who is often talked about, but seldom seen. Preferring late night tides and less crowded locations, you might run into Manny at Block Island, RI one day while a few days later, you might cross paths with him at Cuttyhunk, MA. Always in search of big bass, Manny travels to remote locations along the east coast looking to tangle with big stripers. Considered one of the most aggressive surfcasters today, you will rarely see his light flicker. He'll put it on only if it's really necessary. You will often find him in locations that are better suited for boats then surfcasters. If there is a rock out there that can be mounted, I am convinced that Manny will get on it.

WILLIAM A. MULLER or "Doc" as he is affectionately known, is one of the most prolific saltwater fishing writers and photographers of our generation. He has been an outdoor writer for over 30 years and has contributed countless articles to national, regional, and local publications. He has authored, either in whole or in part, 8 books including his most recent book *Fishing With Bucktails*. In addition to all the praise and awards for his writing skills, the fact remains that "Doc" is one of the most astute students of the sport of surf fishing. He is also one of the most successful surf anglers and has beached many trophy stripers and won 73 first place awards in surf fishing competition. "Doc" has caught three stripers of 50 pounds or more and all were caught on artificial lures, a fact "Doc" uses to encourage new surfcasters to learn to be better anglers by perfecting their skills with lures.

"CRAZY" ALBERTO KNIE is one of the most respected big fish hunters walking the beaches today. Comfortable with a twelve-foot rod in the booming surf as he is with a fly rod or a boat stick, Alberto travels the globe, searching for opportunities to tangle with big fish. You might find him in Canada tossing flies at salmon or teasing marlin off the coast of Costa Rica but he always returns to his true love, the beaches of Long Island, New York. An accomplished seminar speaker and writer, Alberto is also a talented artist and photographer.

BILL WETZEL has been a surf guide for more than a decade. Although you might find him plugging the mud flats on the north shore of Long Island in the spring, or casting along the marshes in Long Island's south shore back bays, Bill's true love is casting from moss-covered rocks found at Montauk Point, New York. A fixture on Montauk beaches for the last twenty years, Bill has introduced many novices and seasoned anglers to the beauty of Montauk's rocky shoreline through his guiding service. Often called "The Hardest Working Guide in the Business", he is relentless in his search for fish for himself and his clients. Bill has penned articles for local fishing magazines and is very active on the fishing seminar circuit. He hosts an Internet forum at www.longislandsurffishing.com on which he shares his knowledge, offers advice and discuses many strategies and techniques that he learned over his long career in the surf.

TABLE OF CONTENTS

INTRODUCTION

Zeno Hromin's new book takes a quantum leap forward, and puts the reader in touch with expert surf fishermen who share with the reader methods of fishing that you may know little or nothing about. As beginners, when we first took up the sport, our goal was to catch a striper. Many of us labored for months, or years, before we caught our first bass. Our next goal was to catch lots of stripers. In this book, Zeno Hromin brings us to the next step. He challenges us to join the hunt for big stripers.

Today, there are more people enjoying surfcasting than ever before in the history of the sport. Many have only recently taken up surf fishing and want to learn everything they can about it. I have gone to seminars and workshops on surf fishing and have been amazed at the crowds in attendance. They come to hear the experts and hang on their every word. This book brings the experts into your home where you can read and re-read each chapter and get something new with each reading. The experts share methods and techniques that some of you have only heard of and did not know how to pursue. All of the writers fish hard and know what they are talking about. Many cut their teeth fishing from the boulders that dot the shore at Montauk. Believe me when I say, if you can fish the surf at Montauk, you can fish anywhere on the coast.

Not only is this a great "how to" book, but it has some entertaining stories that will hold your attention throughout the read. This is Zeno's second book and it's another home run. Never has an angler put so much between the covers of two books. Whether you are an experienced angler or a novice this is a great read for you. If you're an old timer as I am, you can look back to your early days when this book would have been an enormous source of information. It would have put me years ahead of where I was, and it will put you years ahead of where you are today. I am certain that this book will help you put that "bass of your dreams" on the sand.

Tight Lines,
Al Bentsen

CHAPTER ONE

THE ONE THAT GOT AWAY

Memories of the "one that got away" haunt many surfcasters. In some ways, this is what makes us intensify our efforts and increase our determination. We seek redemption and validation as fishermen and most of all, "one more shot" at that dream striper.

You will find few who will admit to losing a big fish as a direct result of "operator error." We usually chalk it up to the strength and power of the striped bass rather than blaming it on ourselves. What follows may sound like blasphemy to you since we are supposed to be experts at all things fishing. Most times it is our fault! Bad knots are primary culprits, along with dull hooks, improperly set drags and frayed leaders. When hooked up to a good fish, hooting, hollering and adopting the general posture of "look at me", is rarely a recipe for success. Neither is wasting precious moments when you should be concentrating on the task at hand. I have done some remarkably dumb things over the years so I should know. Many years ago, when I was full of piss and vinegar, and I thought I knew it all, I received a lesson that I will never forget as long as I live. In my youthful exuberance, I was not content with fishing just one rod. Looking for an edge over my friends I talked myself into plugging with one rod while setting another one in a sand spike with a chunk. I figured I was increasing my chances by using this approach. Little did I know that instead of doing one thing, and doing it well, I wasn't doing either one right.

One fateful night after casting a bunker chunk into the surf, I placed the rod in an open-faced aluminum spike. I then walked back to my truck, which was parked about twenty yards away and grabbed a plugging rod from the roof rack. Fearful of crossing over the line on my chunking rod, I moved twenty yards away, and started casting into the night. Small blues were running in the surf, and they made my bait rod shake with numerous and frequent jerks. Of course, by the time I would run to my rod the fish would be gone and so would the bait. After about an hour of this silliness, the tide had reached the slack period, and the blues moved off in search of more fertile hunting grounds. I was relieved, as I got tired of replacing bait. I impaled a large bunker head with about two inches of meat attached to it, and lobbed it into the water. I was hoping that the head would discourage the small bluefish hits, which it did. Now I could plug with less distraction, and at least some sense of concentration.

What snapped me out of it was the sound of my rod banging against the aluminum spike. By the time I realized what was happening, my rod was doubled over like a pretzel. It appeared that it would explode at any minute from extreme pressure. I rushed towards my rod, when suddenly the rod lost its bend. I knew from experience, that once a rod loses its bend after a hit, the chances of a fish being attached to the hook are almost nonexistent. I slowed from a run to a walk, and was about 10 yards away from my sand spike. My rod, which was now leaning away from the water, suddenly catapulted from the sand spike and fell onto the sand. I watched in horror, almost frozen in my steps, as the rod was dragged into the water. Within seconds, it disappeared in the surf, while I frantically tried to find it. With tears running down my face, I cast a bucktail where I thought the rod might be. I let the bucktail sink to the bottom and then dragged it through the sand. Suddenly I felt weight on the other end! My moment of exuberance was quickly replaced with a sense of disappointment, as I pulled a large, croaking sea robin into the wash. He was attached to the bucktail not my missing rod. I never did find that rod, and this is one of the reasons why you'll never find me on the beach with a spiked rod. This experience left a bad taste in my mouth, and taught me a valuable, and

Hooking a big bass is only half the battle. Landing it can often be just as challenging.

Leaving a rod unattended can have disastrous consequences. Most seasoned anglers hold their rods at all times when fishing bait.

very expensive lesson about the ability and strength of big fish. However, it wasn't the most painful lesson in my life.

My greatest failure, something that haunts me to this day, happened many years ago, while I was still living in a small port in Croatia on the Adriatic Sea. One of the benefits of growing up on a small island off the coast of Croatia was that every household was either on the water or within a view of it. Boats were the primary means of transportation for even mundane tasks such as shopping or a doctor visit. As a result, most of the towns on Croatian islands were built within a few hundred yards of the shoreline.

Catching fish on my own, however enthralling, paled in comparison to the excitement I felt when my grandpa would return from one of his fishing trips. His two brothers would often join him on these three or four-day excursions. Neither men were particularly crazy about fishing but they would go because it meant money in their pockets and some fresh filets for their families. I would be shaking with excitement and would jump on the bow of the boat, as soon as it got close, while my grandfather was tying off the boat to the dock. Then, I would make a beeline for the stern to see what was in the homemade cooler. There might be giant sea rays

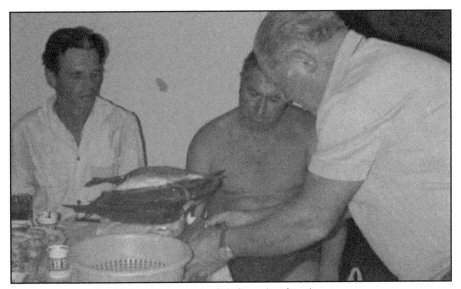

My late grandfather Vinko weighing the fish for sale after the trip.

with long poisonous tails, ugly but delicious scorpion fish, large red snappers, giant eels and massive sand sharks. How I yearned to accompany them on their journeys to far away locations, where giant fish roamed and dolphins swam playfully around the boat. I would soon find out that these trips were hard work and very little fun.

One day when my grandfather had loaded the boat with ice and bait, both of my uncles cancelled at the last minute, and my grandmother suggested he take me with him. He just grunted something under his breath, and before I knew it, I was sitting on the bow of the boat, on the way to the fishing grounds.

The first day was uneventful. My grandfather stood on the stern under a canopy, while I stood in the anchor hatch on the bow, baking in the sun. By the time we finished up in the evening, you could fry an egg on my back, I was burnt that badly. At dusk we anchored in a small, uninhabited harbor. Dinner consisted of fried Spam, fresh salted tomatoes and a bowl of homegrown salad with mixed vegetables. Of course, this was floating in a generous mix of homemade vinegar and olive oil.

After dinner, he would cut large chunks of squid, and sardine, while I impaled them on the hooks of a long-line. Our long-line was a crude contraption compared to modern long-lines that are used with winches and clips. It was made out of heavy rope, tied to a long leader with hooks every few yards. A square box with hundreds of little grooves, made by a hacksaw on the top of the box, held the long line. As you would pull the long-line, the rope would go into the box, while the monofilament leaders would be jammed into the narrow grooves on the top of the box. This kept the long-line untangled and ready to use. After we finished tending to the baited hooks we retreated to our bunks for some shuteye.

To give you a better understanding of what was about to transpire, I feel a need to put this event in the context in which it happened. Unlike modern long-lines, which are pulled in by a winch, my grandfather pulled his in by hand. At the same time, he would place the rope back into the box, remove any bait from the hook, and reinsert the leaders back into the grooves on the box. This meant that my job was to run the boat without cutting across the long-line, as he couldn't do both things. That part I could handle, but since my uncles weren't there, I also inherited the job as a gaff man. I prayed hard that my services wouldn't be needed, as I had never handled a gaff before.

We came up on the buoy around 9 A.M. On the first few hundred feet of long-line, we found a few small red snappers and some strange bottom dwellers. Suddenly, I noticed my grandfather tense up, and slow down his rhythm to a steadier and more gradual retrieve. He could feel something banging against the rope but it was still too far down the long-line to see. I knew he was hoping for a large sand shark or a sea ray. Instead, the crystal clear water revealed a giant silvery shape. At first I thought we were pulling up a refrigerator door, but then I realized it was a fish as it started to circle around the rope. "Darn it," my grandfather said, "it's not spent yet. Put the engine in neutral, and grab the gaff." I struggled with shaky hands trying to budge the large clutch, but the big plastic ball that was attached to a steel rod kept slipping in my sweaty hand. Finally I managed to budge it, threw it in reverse, and then quickly into a neutral to slow down the boat's forward progress. I grabbed a homemade gaff, which was made out of three large shark hooks attached to a broom handle.

For the first time in my life I saw fear in my grandfather's eyes. His "can-do" attitude, which was a big part of his personality, evaporated and was replaced by beads of sweat running down his forehead. I knew he wanted to hand off the long-line to me and grab the gaff, but he knew that

I did not have the strength to hold onto it. Not with a big fish attached to it! Without uttering a word, we both knew what was at stake. The firm white flesh of this monster was much sought after fare by the restaurants my grandfather supplied. It was easily worth two months of his small pension.

His strokes got shorter as he was trying not to spook the fish, which was now only ten feet under the boat. The fish either sensed the presence of the boat or did not care for the bright sunlight glistening above. Suddenly, it started to act very agitated. Sensing impending doom, I moved closer to my grandfather, leaning over the side of the boat. The fish was now circling the long line, and it was heading right for me. I lunged at it with the gaff, and firmly impaled it in the fish's broad shoulders. Mayhem ensued, as the fish's large tail began to beat the water to a froth.

The frayed leader was the first to go, and now I was holding this brute with no margin for error. My grandfather quickly tied the long line to the boat, and rushed to help. The massive weight of the fish was pulling me over the side and in order to get some leverage I stuck my bare legs under the wooden bench that was running along the side of the boat. I felt a sharp pain in my shin. My leg was pressed against a red-hot exhaust pipe, and soon the smell of burning flesh filled the air. In unbearable pain, I dropped the gaff in the water. The fish floated on its side beside the boat. My grandfather lunged at it and grabbed it by its tail. The size of the fish, gravity and slime did their thing and I watched the broom like tail slip through my grandfather's clenched fists. The fish was motionless for a moment. Then it slowly disappeared into the ocean depths with the gaff still attached to its side.

I sat down in disbelief and started to cry. Partly from the pain in my now blistered leg, but more because of what I had done. My grandfather said nothing. He sat next to me, put his arm around my shoulder and began to sob along with me. He never could hold back his tears when he saw me cry. We never caught anything close to that size in the following years, and when my grandfather passed suddenly years later, he left a big void in my life.

I never did tell him how sorry I was. Grandfather, if you are reading this in St. Peter's library in Heaven, I promise you I'll hang onto the gaff the next time we meet.

As you can see, losing a big fish is a traumatic experience, regardless of your age. If you haven't experienced the pain of losing a big fish, you probably haven't fished long enough. I don't consider it a failure, I think of it more as a right of passage for any budding surfcaster. Hey, the fish has to win the battle sometimes; otherwise the moment we hooked into a fish would be the end of our quest. The fight, the sound of a singing drag, battling rough surf or steering the fish away from

Loosing a big fish is always a traumatic experience, regardless of your age.

obstructions are all an integral part of surfcasting. For surfcasters, the hook-up is just the beginning of a battle of wills with a powerful and crafty adversary. Will she run towards that big boulder and try to cut you off? Will she bury her nose into the bottom trying to dislodge the hook or will she just smoke the drag, while you hold on for dear life?

Surfcasters are the epitome of fishing warriors. Like soldiers ready for combat, we stand in the pounding surf or perched on a slimy rock, casting our offering into the darkness. Our reward is not measured in the size or number of the fish we catch! We rejoice in the beauty that is in every wave that folds onto itself. We are thrilled by the sight of a striper gliding gracefully through a cresting wave. And yes, the fish will win the battle sometimes, but as sure as the sun will rise tomorrow, we will come back to the scene of the heartbreak and ask the fishing gods for a chance at redemption.

CHAPTER TWO

BECOMING A BIG FISH HUNTER

Catching large striped bass while your feet are firmly planted on the shore, might be one of the most difficult tasks to accomplish for any type of saltwater angler. So many variables are working against us. The inability to cover a lot of different spots quickly is one. Unlike boat anglers who rarely give much thought to getting a line snagged on an obstruction, barnacle covered rocks have shredded many surfcaster's dreams of hoisting up a trophy striper. Surfcasters are constantly challenged by the conditions that surround them, from man-made obstacles like slippery jetties to rough surf, courtesy of King Neptune. From the moment they bury a hook in a striper's jaw, the battle of wills ensues. The fish immediately tries to wrap a line around any obstruction where a decent amount of pressure will part the line. The surfcaster does his or her best to prevent this from occurring, by using a properly set drag, and by keeping tension on the fish with the rod. Even if the angler succeeds in keeping a large bass away from

Landing a big fish on a jetty can be a difficult experience, even under optimal conditions.

Rough surf conditions can be our worst enemy when landing a big bass.

boulders, bridge abutments, mussel beds or any other place where a bass might head for safety, he or she still has to deal with landing the fish.

I am convinced that more fish are lost during the landing process than they are during the initial fight. If you are a jetty jock, you know what dangers await you, as you bring that big fish close to the rocks. You know that you might get one shot at landing the fish before your line is scuffed up by the jagged rocks and easily parts.

Even the angler standing on a sandy beach, with no visible obstructions in his way, has a strong adversary to contend with and its name does not have stripes on it. Its name is "Last Wave", although I would argue that "Heartbreaker" is much more fitting. Play your large fish the wrong way and you will experience that last wave exerting tension on your tackle. This is the result of thousands of gallons of rushing water attempting to recede from the beach, back towards the ocean. Many lines have parted right here due to many factors, including line and or knot failure. That last receding wave, with all the pressure it generates, will test your skill and equipment as well as whether or not you have set your drag properly. This is true for days when the surf is calm, and especially true when rough water prevails. Memories of large tails slapping on the dry sand haunt many anglers, who watched a receding wave carry their fish back into the surf. Occurrences such as these happen regularly in the surf, but they do very little to deter us from our quest. I look at them as part of the learning experience, regardless of how painful and heartbreaking it can be. If you are like me, I doubt that you will make the same mistake twice. Any failure which occurred that resulted in the loss of a big fish, has been noted permanently in my brain, hopefully never to be repeated again.

BECOMING A BIG FISH HUNTER

Hunting large stripers from the surf requires a different mindset, on the part of a surfcaster, than just wanting to catch "a fish". It requires attention to detail, frequent references to a logbook carefully kept over the years. It requires a good knowledge of the tides, current and winds. Most importantly, an understanding of how these three natural occurrences will influence water movement in your targeted area. It also requires that you forsake the pleasure of catching many smaller fish for that one shot at the bigger one. You will notice a common thread running through the chapters of this book, written by some of today's most respected surfcasters. They will all gladly spend hours without a bump, in return for that one hit from a large striper. I will not mislead you, this is a lot harder to accomplish than it seems. Most surfcasters have what it takes to target large fish: good tackle, the ability to select great lures, and the knowledge of locations that are known to produce big fish. But most of them will give up on their quest for big stripers after a few hours of fruitless casting, sometimes even much sooner. The call of "saving the night", with fish of any size, becomes too strong to ignore, and they will downsize their lure in order to get that familiar bump.

CAN YOU WALK AWAY?

Another thing to ask yourself is, are you willing to walk away from small fish? Do you have enough strength to walk away from acres of blitzing teen size bass? It sounds very easy to do, but let me assure you, it is not! Seeing every surfcaster with a bend in a rod, even those that have taken up the sport recently, is a hard thing to pass up. You will have to, if you are looking to cull a bigger fish. We all know that smaller fish are much more aggressive than larger ones. The chance of a big fish getting to your lure before their smaller siblings are very slim. If you think you will entice a larger fish, with an above average size lure when fish are feeding actively, you will probably be very disappointed. This seemingly good strategy rarely ever works during a feeding frenzy. Actively feeding fish will hit any lure, regardless of the shape or size. The only way, in my humble opinion, is to walk away from the mayhem, and work the areas the feeding fish have already passed through. Why? Big stripers have a well-documented preference of feeding on scraps left behind by a feeding frenzy whipped up by their smaller siblings, instead of joining in the fray. Methodically and stealthily, they cruise the quiet waters that seem void of life, especially in comparison to the actively feeding fish moving down the beach. They are looking for scraps, half eaten fish chopped by blues, or baitfish that have been wounded by stripers. You'd never know they are there...unless you walk away from the blitz. Many cows have fallen to large metal lip swimmers worked slowly in the areas that blitz fish have abandoned in search of more productive feeding grounds. I often stay in the area well after most surfcasters have jumped in their buggies, and taken off down the beach, following the fish. Often I am rewarded with my biggest fish of the day. I won't lie to you, it is very hard to cast into a seemingly barren ocean while you watch blitz madness a quarter mile down the beach.

RIGHT FRAME OF MIND

That brings me to another requirement for hunting big stripers: determination. I know, we are all determined to catch a big fish. This is why we fish, isn't it? Unfortunately, determination to target large fish greatly differs from willingness to catch fish. You think I am exaggerating? Look around you, and you'll see that many marriages have broken up over fishing. How many surfcasters parted ways with their spouses because they were obsessed about catching school stripers? Not many. Determination means that you will forsake sleep, meals and family time in order to give yourself a fighting chance of catching that cow bass. Extremely rare, are occurrences of large fish charging the surf in broad daylight. They are much more comfortable in deep water rips when the sun is above the horizon. To add insult to injury, they find the hours from midnight to dawn, much more to their liking than any other time period. When everything settles down and the boat traffic has abated, the bass move in under the cover of darkness to feed.

Late night tides are often the best time to tangle with quality stripers.

This obviously presents a huge problem to all those sane people among us, who have to hold down a job in addition to fulfilling our family duties. Too many nights of chasing after these brutes will leave your body hurting, and your mind spinning. Some among us have even more difficulty with these hours than others. Having a desk job is great after a long night. At least you get to plop down in a cushy chair and pretend to be awake. For guys like me that are in construction, where accidents are the norm rather then exception, fishing these types of hours is difficult. Working on a construction site, or operating a motor vehicle in a zombie-like state because of lack of sleep, is a disaster waiting to happen. Not just for you, but also for those people around you, so pick your battles carefully. No fish is worth your life, or the anguish you might cause to another family because you were too tired to function properly. Determination also means sticking with a plan you carefully laid out prior to your trip. It means sticking with that large rigged eel, knowing that you are forsaking the chance of landing many smaller fish. If those around you are all hooked up with school bass on bucktails, are you willing to stay with your nine-inch shad, in order for you to get a shot at the biggest fish in the area? You know as well as I do, that the largest fish in that pod has as much chance of getting to your bucktail ahead of its smaller cousins, as you have of getting a date with a movie starlet. Yeah, it could happen. You could walk out of a Broadway Theater after seeing a show with your girlfriend, and bump into a movie star while crossing the street. You could pick her up off the street, and she could gaze into your eyes, which will cause you to forget you ever had a girlfriend. You'll fly to Las Vegas, get married, move to Malibu, and become a celebrity. It could happen, but it probably won't. In fact, you have a slimmer chance of that large fish getting to your bucktail first, then you becoming George Clooney's neighbor.

Another requirement of being a big fish hunter is willingness to travel. If you think that the big fish will populate the spots that are convenient for you, you'll be sorely disappointed. Yes, there are many well-known locations, which have a tendency to attract large fish year after year. The shores of the Cape Cod Canal come to mind, as do the rocky shorelines of Block Island, Cuttyhunk and Montauk Point. Breachways or inlets along

the striper coast are notorious big fish producers, and attract their share of big fish hunters, as do bridges and their adjoining shorelines. The first thing you will notice, is that all of these spots are strategically located where massive amounts of water, baitfish, and game fish must wrap around them on their migration. All these places share common characteristics. They are all places where a lot of water is being forced through a narrow opening between two points of

My frequent traveling partner, Rob, was rewarded with this mid 30's fish on our recent trip to Cuttyhunk, MA.

land. This in turn creates faster current speeds than you will find along the open beach. But these spots, although consistently more productive than open sand beaches, are not guaranteed to provide you with that fish of your dreams.

I don't suggest you become a report chaser, but you will have to tap into your network of friends and acquaintances, along with other sources of reliable information in order to predict where your best chances are to tangle with big stripers. I am a big believer that these fish move in pods. I am not alone in this belief, as underwater research by well-known experts has come to similar conclusions. They are creatures of habit, and will return to their haunts year after year, but they are also constantly on the move,

Hunting for a big fish often requires traveling on a moments notice.

especially during migration. You can more or less accurately predict when a body of fish in Staten Island, New York this week will reach the confines of Jones or Fire Island inlet on Long Island the following week. This is when a meticulously kept log becomes an invaluable tool for looking up past patterns and occurrences. There are many things from weather patterns to bait availability that will influence their movement and behavior. Your logged entries from the past should give you a pretty good indication as to when your chances of hooking a cow striper might be above average.

It's like a game of chess, you need to plan and think ahead. A good chess player doesn't just make a move. He takes into consideration future moves as well. Big fish don't stop at certain locations and call it home. They will be available for a short period of time and it's absolutely imperative for a surfcaster to find out when this period will present itself in his area. Sometimes, the big fish will show up at the "wrong place and wrong time". Feeding in the daytime sun, or in a warm August surf are exceptions, but they do happen. They don't however happen for no apparent reason. This is a story about determination, readiness, and willingness to travel to catch a big fish. Of course, like all things that happen to me, the tale that follows is full of stupidity, humility, and above all willingness to learn new things. Throw in the mix, the company of a trusted friend, and some nice size linesiders, and I had a night to remember.

DRIVING MR. DAISY

A few years ago, on a scorching hot August morning, I was resting at home, and ingesting painkillers like they were going out of style. I was lying sideways on my couch watching TV, not able to do much more than that. I couldn't do much else, as I had about a dozen stitches in my behind, courtesy of a friendly surgeon who a day earlier, removed a cyst that formed on top of my coccyx bone. Although I was able to sit on cushions, it was very uncomfortable, and I found some relief by lying on my side. My phone rang, and although I really wasn't in the mood to talk to anyone, I took the call after I saw that it was Alberto. For those of you who might not know, Alberto Knie is one of the premier big fish hunters of our generation. The man will travel to the ends of the earth to find what he is after and he never stops fishing. Not for a day! He earns his well-deserved nickname, "Crazy Al". I answered the phone with a "Hello", and Al replied in his signature line, "So?" "So what?" I said, "You called me." I knew Al's playful nature, but today was not the day to be coy with me as I reached for the Vioxx again. "Bubba, I found big fish" he said, "You want to come and play?"

Now big fish and August are not mutually exclusive in my mind. Not that my brain functions on such a high level to begin with, as you will soon find out. After all, Bill Wetzel's big fish strategy, which he outlines in an upcoming chapter, relies heavily on August cow hunting. For me however,

August always meant a 7-foot St Croix, Van Staal 150, half-ounce bubblegum jelly worms, and summer weakfish. I knew full well that there was no way in hell that my wife was going to let me go hop the inlet jetties in my current condition. Of course, Montauk was out of the question, as fishing there is more physically demanding than any place I've ever fished.

I started to quiz Al about his statement, kind of working in the issue that hopping like a goat on Montauk rocks wasn't an option, but he was predictably closed mouthed. He wanted commitment before he divulged any more information. I had no choice but to come clean about the shape I was in, to which he replied "Don't worry, we'll fish sand". "Huh?" I replied, puzzled by what I heard. "You want to fish sand beaches, in the middle of August, in piss warm water?" He filled me in on what he had been doing. My mind wandered off as he was talking. I knew a few guys had posted some big fish pictures on the Internet boards the last few days, which was unusual for August. He informed me that he took those guys out with him, but they turned around and spilled the beans. To add insult to injury, one guy showed up with a hand held GPS; recording the location they were fishing! I put two and two together, and now he had me hooked, and that evening I was driving east to Al's house.

I sat on four thick cushions during this short half hour ride, which seemed much longer this particular day. I had not given much thought to driving for another hour and a half to Montauk, assuming Al was going to do it in his truck. I buzzed his bell, and he came out with his chunking stick .He put it on my rack, threw his gear in the back, sat on the passenger side, and said "Lets go". Before I even had a chance to protest about my sore butt, he passed out and was snoring. I knew he had put in all-nighters the last few nights, but this was something I wasn't planning on.

The ride was uneventful with Al soundly asleep, and me fidgeting on the seat in discomfort. Finally, we arrived in Montauk, and I parked at the 4-wheel drive entrance. As soon as the engine shut off, Al awoke and looked at his watch." Good" he said, "we have plenty of time before the fish show up". At this point it was around 9 P.M., and the sun had dipped beyond the western horizon. I grabbed my flashlight and tire gauge, and started to release the air out of the tires, getting them ready for soft, summer sand. As I bent down to the front tire and unscrewed the cap, I looked at the back of my truck with puzzlement. The truck was leaning to one side. Walking towards the back, I spotted the problem immediately. The back tire was emptied out naturally, courtesy of a long nail! Al suggested we drive a few hundred yards to a gas station for better lighting. Although the station was closed, the lights were usually left on during the night. We wobbled slowly on the main road, and pulled into the station only to find that the lighting left a lot to be desired.

To understand what was about to transpire I feel I need to make you aware of a few things. First, I've changed plenty of flat tires on trucks and cars over the years. However, I never had a spare tire mounted under the chassis, as I did now on my old Ford Explorer. Neither one of us had a clue how to release the tire to the ground. I placed a towel on the ground, and crawled under the truck. With a screwdriver and a pair of pliers, I hammered at the butterfly clamp that held the tire. The clamp was

spinning all right, but the tire wasn't descending. At this point I felt blood gushing through my stitches, as I hammered at the clamp. Al stood above me with a flashlight, with a big grin on his face. My painful predicament was not what he was worried about. Instead, he feared he was going to drain his batteries in the flashlight. Oh yeah, and the fact we might miss out on some fish. I have never come

Making slight adjustments to your terminal tackle can be the difference between success and failure.

closer to wanting to choke another human being! First, he makes me drive for two hours with a dozen stitches in my butt, and now this! Finally, the small part of my brain, which occasionally needs a reboot to function properly kicked in. I got up and searched the truck for a owner's manual. After consulting a diagram in the manual, I realized that behind the back seat there was a rod, which was used to lower the spare tire from underneath the truck. You had to stick the rod into the small hole, located in the rear above the tire. A few cranks of that rod and the tire started to descend. At this point I would have been happy to just change the tire and go back home. I didn't care about fishing any more; I was tired, in pain, and out of painkillers and patience.

After I got the tire loose, we replaced the flat one quickly, and got onto the beach. Al had me driving close to the cliffs, instead of close to the water, as I am accustomed to. I soon realized he was looking for land markings. Due to the flat-water conditions, and pitch-black darkness, most of the shoreline looked the same. As we drove, he occasionally would point his flashlight into the vegetation that we were passing. "Stop" he said." Go back five feet, I think we are there," he added. I slowly backed up the truck, and low and behold, Al found his land marking.

We got out of the truck and he asked me "Did you bring bank sinkers like I told you?" "Yes" I replied, not telling him I brought them with me only because he asked. I had no intention of actually using them. Let's get real! Whom do you know that uses bank sinkers in the surf! In some ways I was hoping that the fish would be a no-show. This way, we could cut the trip short. I was in no mood for chatting. I attached a 6-ounce pyramid sinker, away from Al's prying eyes, and impaled a big chunk of bunker onto the hook. I walked into the water, loaded up my conventional stick, and lobbed the bait. To be honest, there really was no reason to expect anything extraordinary on this particular location. Maybe Al had different wind conditions and higher surf the last few nights but this night, there was gentle, calm surf present. As I looked down the beach on both sides, nothing about this particular location seemed that fishy to me. Calm surf, very high water temperatures, and no distinctive structure had me cursing under my breath, and longing for my warm bed. Al was still setting up his rig as I was walking out of the water. I was holding my rod on my shoulder, and before I had a chance to turn towards the water the rod was almost yanked out of my hands. Performing a pirouette, although much less gracefully than a figure skater, I turned around quickly and set the hook. My rod bent in an arc and I knew I had a good fish on. When I toss bait I use a Lamiglas rod made out of the 136 1MH blank. It's a wonderful rod that will handle a 12-ounce sinker, and bunker head without a problem, but it does take a decent fish to put a nice bend in it. Al walked up with a big smile on his face and said, "I told you they are here". The problem was, although I could feel this fish pump, I could not move it. The fish was stuck behind something and although I could feel it, I could not budge it. Al walked over and asked, "You used bank sinkers, right?" I put my head down, and replied in a sheepishly quiet voice." No". He smirked and said "What?" I told you to bring bank sinkers. Do you think I did that to bust your chops? There is a small mussel bed that has been covered by sand for years. A recent storm moved the sand off the bed, and unearthed boulders and mussels. This brought in porgy's that are feeding on mussels. On their tails are large stripers, and they are feasting on them. They are smart, and they will take you in the rocks almost immediately."

I felt my feet sinking in the sand even further as I listened for more words of wisdom of how to get out of this situation. Al took a minute to make sure the stuff he was saying was sinking in. He said, "Tighten up the drag and pull. The fish finder that holds the sinker is the weakest link, and hopefully it will break before your line does". I did as he said, and started walking backwards while holding a thumb on my spool to prevent slippage. I felt something give but I wasn't sure if it was the line or the sinker. I was relieved to find that the fish was still attached to the line, but I was also surprised by lack of effort on its part.

A few moments later a fish in the high 20's lay on the sand motionless, spent from fighting to get out of the rock pile. It took a long time to revive it, but I was committed to the task, as I felt bad that my own ignorance led to this. After a few minutes, I was encouraged when I felt its strength coming back to its body, and after some gentle cradling in the water, the striper slowly glided away. I stood over it and watched it weave through the calm surf. I re-rigged with a bank sinker this time, and made another lob. It must have hit a fish in the head, because I did not even make a single step towards the shore, and I was already hooked up. I felt the sinker banging amongst the rocks, but it didn't get stuck. This fish was slightly smaller than the previous one but still well over 20 lbs. For August, when any weakfish over five pounds will get my adrenaline pumping, this was an incredible occurrence considering the scenery, time of the year, water temps and gentle surf. It proves the point that bigger fish will not necessarily be put off by conditions, if there is an ample supply of bigger bait in the area.

In the next hour, I landed another eight fish, all between 20 and 30 lbs. In the meantime, Alberto, who was only about ten yards away, had only a single fish. He told me that the same thing happened during the last few nights and this is why he had me back up my truck five feet. He said that if your bait were only a few feet away from the mussel beds, your score would decrease dramatically. I suggested that he move closer to me, but he said something that made me question his sanity. "I am going for a power nap," he declared, adding, "Big cows will be here at 2:30 A.M." Considering it was about midnight, and I was having one of the best August nights in a long time, I wasn't moving. In fact, I doubt you could have moved me with a crane. Long forgotten was the pain in my behind, or the disastrous tire changing experience.

Having a thorough knowledge of the location you are targeting is a prerequisite for success.

While Al napped, I managed to catch a fish or get a hit, on just about every cast. He woke up at 2:15 A.M., and asked what was happening. I told him I stopped counting fish after a dozen, but in the last hour, the size of the fish got noticeably smaller. Instead of 20 to 30 pound fish, now I was catching 12 to 17 pound fish. Not bad but hey, even an incompetent googan like me gets greedy once in awhile.

Al said nothing, and walked to the back of the truck. He stripped all the line off his reel, and replaced it with fresh monofilament from a large spool. Once the rigging was completed, he spiked the rod and said "Ten minutes to show time". "Yeah, right", I said to myself. Not wanting to admit, I was kind of glad he slept through this great bite. Otherwise, I'd have to share the fish with him. Hey, I love him like a brother, but I want to catch every fish that swims in the ocean! A few minutes later, he cut a big chunk of fresh bunker, and put it on the hook. He walked to the water, this time a little closer to me than where he was originally before his nap. He tossed the bait out, engaged the reel and remained motionless. I chalked it up to him not being fully awake. In the split second that it took me to kneel down, and get another piece of bait, everything changed. Al's body was now leaning backwards, almost diagonally to the sand, and his rod was bent in a huge arc. "Son of a gun" I said to myself, in disbelief. Al slid his bass onto the sand, and I immediately realized that it was bigger than anything I caught all night. Sure enough, after a quick scale measurement, it weighed around 34 pounds; I made a cast with my chunk, and cursed under my breath. A guy sleeps most of the night; wakes up, and on a first cast, nails the biggest fish of the night! A good thump on my rod brought me back to reality. I followed the fish by lowering my rod tip, and as the line came tight, I set the hook hard, then one more time for good measure. It was evident almost immediately that this fish was larger than any I had caught all night. It peeled the drag in three different sequences, but it eventually succumbed to the pressure of my bent graphite rod. Once I got it in the wash, I grabbed it by the gills and dragged it onto dry sand. My Boga Grip showed 33 pounds, just a shade smaller than Al's fish. At this point Al was back into the water, but now nervously fidgeting. He asked for the size of my fish, but said nothing more. Ten minutes later, he walks up to me with his hook attached to the guide and declared the bite to be over.

With that, he placed the rod on the roof rack, got into the passenger seat and started nodding off. There was no way I was going to pack it in now, I said to myself. After all, I just nailed my biggest fish of the night not more than ten minutes ago. Would you believe me if I told you that I stood there for the next three hours without as much as a bump! Not even the skates were interested in what I was offering. The sleeping beauty woke up around 5:30 A.M., and immediately asked about the action. Grinning mischievously, he expressed a strong desire for some coffee. I didn't mind that one bit, as the pain in my behind was getting unbearable. I hadn't slept all night and the last time I lay down was under the truck, trying to remove the spare tire.

DOES LUCK PLAY A PART?

As you can see, it took about all the strength and patience I had in me to get through this night. Yes, the results were excellent, considering the time of the season, but they did not occur because of luck. The catch that we put together that night was the result of meshing together knowledge, reports and extreme familiarity with the structure we were targeting. Al has logged many nights in this area, getting the bite down to a science. Anyone who can predict the time when the biggest fish of the night will make an appearance and be confident that it will occur within a twenty minute period, has skills way beyond my comprehension. To be right, and have fish show up right on time is, however, not a result of some voodoo science. It has more to do with keeping a detailed log, and most of all, putting the time in on the beach.

You'll find out in upcoming chapters that luck is not a part of a mindset that these extremely successful big fish hunters count on. My late grandfather was adamant that each man makes his own luck. Yes, there will be those times when someone will catch a monster on a rotten clam, in broad daylight. In addition, there will be guys who will show up on the beach, and on their first cast, catch a fish of a lifetime while those around him, who have been plugging for hours with no results, look on in disbelief. It can, it will and it does happen every year. But I didn't write this book and go through the pain of typing with my index finger, in addition to persuading some great fishermen to share their knowledge, to tell you that you should be counting on luck. To be constantly successful in catching large striped bass, it will take more than luck. It actually might take more than you are willing to give, which is ok. Many surfcasters are perfectly content with catching fish on a consistent basis, and feel no need to target large fish specifically. This doesn't make them any less of a person or angler in my book. I am a big believer that each person has to find their own comfort zone, putting the family needs first, and then satisfying their own desires second. The ability to travel on the first sign of a nor'easter howling up the coast, casting live or rigged eels, or big chunks of bait, is not everyone's forte. Neither is targeting fish during the time when most others are sound asleep. You will have to make sacrifices in order to increase the size of the fish you catch. You will not catch them consistently with small lures, and you will not do it often in daylight, and you certainly will not catch one from your couch!

CHAPTER THREE

BAIT, MOONS & TIDES

In this book you will find a few common threads running through the chapters, namely the determination to search for big fish, frequent references to moon periods and tidal currents as important factors when targeting large fish and the importance of the presence of large baitfish. The latter point is certainly something that will be repeated quite often by the contributors in this book. Find big baitfish and your chances of hooking up with a cow striper will greatly increase. In addition, when using big lures that imitate big baitfish, you will find that they will take most of the hits from smaller fish out of the equation. This might sound like a simplistic strategy but I assure you, it works.

After all, do you really expect to see a sumo wrestler at your neighborhood salad bar? If not, then why expect large stripers to get excited over small baitfish? Let me give you an example of the great action that occurred on New Jersey oceanfront beaches over the last few years. Large bunker made a return appearance once again on the New Jersey beaches this spring. Vast schools of adult bunker were corralled by cow stripers and pinned between the jetties that dot the New Jersey shoreline. Even novices were hooking up with 30 and 40-pound bass with regularity and becoming instant Internet heroes overnight. In many ways, I am thrilled that my friends were having the time of their lives, as they were casting large pencil poppers into schools of oversized stripers. If you are not aware, New Jersey surfcasters have been on the receiving end of some very poor fishing in past years. These hard working surf rats have seen their jetties buried with sand and they have lost a lot of access along the shore. Added to that is the fact that for many years the migrating fish simply passed by offshore, never coming into the surf zone. Thus, the lack of baitfish and structure to attract and hold stripers was the primary culprit. Much of this has to do with large commercial vessels netting massive quantities of adult bunker in the open ocean over the years. They use this oily baitfish for commercial purposes, including fertilizers, paint and the production of

These bunker were pushed against the shore by feeding gamefish resulting in a memorable day for those lucky enough to be present.

omega oil supplements. However, in recent years this practice has been banned in New Jersey, and suddenly New Jersey surfcasters are the recipients of a trophy striper bonanza. Granted, the bass are migrating and the run only lasts for a week or two and is unpredictable based on weather patterns, but, my Lord, the action it produces! Imagine every angler on a jetty hooked up simultaneously with 30-pound class stripers or better!

To add insult to injury to all of us who were not able to cash in on this bonanza, for whatever reason, all this action occurred in broad daylight. Now if you think that this is a historically unusual occurrence you will have to brush up on your striper facts. Similar action occurs in other places and has occurred in recent years.

Cape Cod Canal has a short window in spring when large stripers are feasting on herring, as they do at herring runs throughout New England. Narragansett Bay in Rhode Island was absolutely on fire last year with trophy size stripers feasting on adult bunker. Let us not forget the heydays of Block Island and Cape Cod beaches twenty years ago when schools of extremely large sand eels flooded the surf thus contributing to some of the most spectacular fishing anyone can recall.

As I am writing this, in early June 2008, Long Island south shore and

Montauk beaches have been unusually quiet thus far. Not deserted, but the action is certainly not up to par in comparison to past years and of course not up to our expectations which, by the way, are always based on past experience. Voodoo and wishful thinking is better left to charlatans so stick to your log and your past experience if you are looking to decipher the secret of hooking up with cows consistently. Then of course, heed the advice of the very successful surfcasters in this book. Yeah, I guess you can listen to me too, but only if you must.

All kidding aside, the main reason why the beaches of Long Island are not producing their share of cow stripers is simple. Migrating fish that are moving from their southern wintering grounds, or descending from the Hudson River after they spawn make Jamaica Bay their first stop in our waters. Located on the eastern tip of New York City, (behind the Rockaway Beaches) this rich back bay ecosystem has in recent years become a major staging ground for adult bunker. When stripers enter the bay, they feed on these baitfish with gusto. The action is fast and furious, but after a week or two of binge feeding, they will start migrating eastward. For years this worked like clockwork. In fact, many cow hunters claimed they could predict with regularity how many days it would take before freshly arrived stripers from Jamaica Bay migrated to Jones Inlet, then to Fire Island inlet and so on. This year, 2008,

Many lures can be effective when big bass are feeding on bunker but none are deadlier then a large pencil popper.

their mathematical calculations failed them, and left many surfcasters scratching their heads. Instead of spending days in Jamaica Bay, as they expected, they were there for weeks. On top of that, there has only been a small trickle of big fish leaving the bay. The major body of these larger striped bass stayed in Jamaica bay for a long time, compared to the past. They came, they saw the bunker and they never left! It has gotten so bad that many have lost their patience, and started to drive to New York City in order to fish Jamaica Bay. Some have even resorted to parking along John F. Kennedy Airport in order to sneak onto the back bay marshes that surround the airport. Needless to say, Homeland Security personnel are not amused one bit. It is hard to explain to non-fishing folk that you have the "big fish shakes". Trying to explain this to Homeland Security personnel is not something I would recommend.

As you see, big bait is what makes the cow striper world go round. Yes, you might get lucky and catch one at any old time on any bait or lure and some people do. In addition, yes, a small lure is the one on which, according to legend, Al McReynolds landed his world record bass from a jetty in Atlantic City, New Jersey in 1982. So you too might get lucky one day. However, if you want to catch big fish consistently or at least on a regular basis, I suggest you get in tune with your large resident baitfish population. Stalk them, pay attention to their movements and observe their behavior. I can guarantee you, that if you do, they, and not Internet reports, will lead you to the Promised Land.

SMALL BAIT

I already outlined my belief that big baitfish holds the key to catching large stripers. You might be wondering what do you do when you do not see large baitfish in your area. Are your chances of catching a big bass significantly reduced? Absolutely not! In fact, the presence of small bait during a particular time of the year can draw big stripers in the area. I love big bait and will often go out of my way to find them, but small baitfish, in my opinion, is what keeps the resident population of stripers in the area.

The lack of sand eels, or spearing early in the year will generally result in poor fishing in the spring. Migrating stripers have very little reason to take up residence in your local waters if baitfish are not plentiful or even worse, nonexistent. The second reason that small bait is important is more complicated, but it's directly correlated to the presence of big stripers in any particular area. "You said you want big baitfish and now you are contradicting yourself," you might say. Let me explain exactly what I am talking about.

In early fall you will find a great concentration of small bait, either ready to migrate or already on their way. If you are lucky you might find hordes of stripers

Don't be disappointed finding small bait in the spring. They will draw bigger bait into the area attracting large stripers.

and blues feasting on these baitfish. Small bay anchovies, peanut bunker, or sand eels are the primary culprits for inspiring blitz conditions. Most of the stripers you will catch will vary in size from year to year, but most of the time teen size stripers will be the largest ones caught. I doubt you'll find trophy stripers under these conditions, even if you follow the "fish the area after the blitz" approach. Plentiful small bait and aggressive small stripers, is not the scenario big bass prefer to feed in.

Now let's backtrack to spring. During this time of the year, particularly in late spring you'll have these same type of baitfish present, except they will be even smaller in size. Sand eels, spearing and massive hatches of grass shrimp can be found in the surf zone. Unlike in the fall, when bass and blues are generally not competing with other species for the same food, spring has a different dynamic happening under the surface.

Ocean herring, large shad, mackerel and squid populate the suds and back bays, searching for food. Guess what type of food they find in the shallow waters? The same ones the stripers are feeding on. School stripers that often dominate the spring action are generally too small to go after these large baitfishes. However their large siblings, the ones that keep you awake at night, will be on the prowl and feeding on these large species. They don't call herring and shad "bass candy" for nothing and bass did not earn their nickname "squid hounds" for no apparent reason either. These same occurrences repeat themselves late in the fall, but by the time they do, often in late November, a lot of surf rats have already put away their gear. Like everything else in this great sport that we enjoy so much, there are no guaranties, but when and if herring and squid make an appearance along the beaches in late fall, it can often result in some of the best fishing of the year. Many cows will move into the surf zone from deep ocean waters and deep holes in the back bays to feed on large baitfish.

For this particular reason, I approach spring cow hunting differently than I do fall fishing. In the fall, if I am consistently catching small fish through the tide, I have very little confidence that big fish will hit my lure. In fact, I'll often walk away from these fish in search of larger fish. There is a saying, "never leave fish to find fish" In this case you'd be better off doing just that if you are looking for a larger fish. Mind you, this is not because I am some kind of a snob who looks down on catching small fish. Lord knows that there are too many among us who feel this way. Thankfully I am not one of them. I take pleasure out of each and every fish I catch, be that bass, blues or weakfish.

For me, the actual act of hooking up is less important, than what precedes that event. Careful planning, attention to wind, tides, moon periods, currents and proper lure or bait presentation is what I enjoy. The actual act of landing a fish is just a reward for my preparation. Usually in the fall, I start to feel the season slipping away from me. With every passing cold front, the water temperature dips a little. More and more baitfish are leaving our bays and on their tails are stripers and blues feeding heavily as they migrate also. During this time, I feel the urge to seek out bigger fish because I know that a few bad days of unwelcome weather or a hurricane passing hundreds of miles offshore can put the kibosh on the season.

As I mentioned before, the fact that small stripers and large baitfish feed on the same small sand eels, spearing and other small baitfish, is a very significant event in the spring. The difference between spring and fall lies in the feeding habits of large bass. In the fall, the bait is generally more plentiful and larger than the spring. For example, young of the year bluefish, (also known as snappers) grow rapidly during summer months. So do baby bunker, juvenile weakfish and many other species. If we assume that large stripers prefer bigger baitfish to smaller ones, then we can conclude that they have a much bigger selection of baitfish to choose from in the fall. Unlike in fall, when I will often walk away from smaller fish, I welcome them with open arms in spring. Why? Since small fish are feeding on small bait and if herring, shad or squid are in the area, they will also feed on the same small baitfish along with the stripers. This in turn will get large stripers interested and drawn into the area. Our job is to choose a proper lure or bait to induce a strike. With this in mind, go with large nine-inch shads, big plugs and rigged or live eels. The last thing you want to do is toss a four-inch swimmer and connect with school bass on every cast. Not that there is anything wrong with that and if that floats your boat, by all means enjoy yourself. Just remember why large stripers are in the area to begin with. They are not there because of spearing, or small sand eels, but because of the baitfish that feed on them. Choose your weapon carefully. Yes, it's maddening to toss a big shad and fail to hook up, while everyone around you is bailing schoolies. It is the price you will have to pay and every cow hunter is aware of that, so instead of moaning and pouting just accept it. You'll sleep better at night knowing you gave yourself the best chance for success.

MOON PERIODS

A lot is being said and written about the importance of fishing around new and full moon periods each month. The general consensus in the surf fishing community is that a few days before, and after each period, are the best times to target large stripers. Is this based on actual facts or is it another old wives tale? After all, if most guys target these periods, and slack off the rest of the month, wouldn't that skew landings towards these times of the month?

New moon periods are the favorite times of big fish hunters. Darker than normal nights and faster currents are some of the reasons why.

To be honest, I never really liked fishing around a full moon. The bright nights were never my favorite time to fish. A new moon, on the other hand, although causing similar effects in terms of tidal height, gets me very excited. The primary reason for my feelings is the darkness associated with a new moon. Full moon trophy hunting is for the most part a boatmen's paradise, as the deep rips they fish are a lot less influenced by the bright nights. Shore bound anglers usually wish for some cloud cover to minimize the brightness of a full moon. The increased, or decreased light levels are not the only things that are important during these moon periods. The increased current flow that is associated with new and full moon periods have a tendency to disrupt and change fishing in an area. It is not unusual to find a place barren of bait and predators, in an area that featured both before these periods occurred. Consequently, you might find that after the moon period has abated, a new body of fish will move into the area. This is what makes these periods very important.

I've had a few good nights fishing around full moon periods over the years but they pale in comparison to how many bad nights I've had. New moon, and the darkness associated with it, has been much more productive for me.

These lunar periods occur each month of the year, but I find that June, October and November to be most productive when it comes to targeting large fish. You might find better success during different times of the year as water temperatures, and migration patterns are different in the northern range of the striper population, than they are in the southern ones.

During full and new moon periods the current flows are faster than normal. This often requires changes in presentation, at least when using lures. I prefer to have my lures as close to the bottom as possible most of the time. During moon periods, I find it even more important. Faster than normal currents usually mean that larger fish will be hugging the bottom and seeking obstructions to break up the current. Remember, regardless of how small the obstruction is, the water will still divert around it. There are no obstructions that I am aware of that exist in the mid-water column or on the surface. This generally leads to using heavy lures that will get close to the bottom quickly, with the least water resistance. Keeping lures in the bottom half of the water column has worked best for me over the years.

I spend most of my time fishing around inlets, and I'll usually wait until a few days have passed, after the new moon, before I start targeting large fish. The reason for this is that on the actual night of a new moon, the tide is at its highest. As the incoming tide floods the back bay marshes, it pulls out all the dead grass from the marshes as it recedes. This great natural occurrence is God's way of keeping back bay marshes vibrant, and healthy, but unfortunately, this dead grass usually finds its way to the inlets, making fishing difficult at best. I find a day or two after the new moon has passed to be the most productive, based on my logs but I have to warn you, I also fish these periods harder than any others during the month.

All this talk about currents, speeds and water movement has you probably asking, "What if I don't want to toss jigs in fast water"? Actually, you don't have to. Heck, the best way to catch a trophy striper is with a chunk of bunker. Bottom fishing under normal conditions only requires the right amount of lead to hold bottom. So, current speed will have very little effect on your game. What about periods of slack and slower moving currents? We are constantly told that stripers feed best when the current is moving, and they do. But in my opinion, the slower current periods that occur around slack water, during low and high tide, are the most productive times to catch a large bass. I based my opinion on my own personal experience, conversations with very successful anglers and by noting the catches of my friends.

CHANGE IS GOOD

You might question why I hold the time around slack water in such high regard? After all, aren't the stripers supposed to use currents to their benefit, by using their stronger swimming ability to ambush the baitfish? Yes, there is a lot of truth to that. But big stripers don't necessarily operate like their smaller siblings. If they did, you'd find them at every tide feeding along side of their smaller siblings. But you don't, do you? We do tend to categorize big fish as "lazy" feeders, not willing to exert too much energy during their feeding process. I think lazy is the wrong term. Opportunistic is much closer to the truth, in my opinion. Fish do not like to expend more energy than that which is contained in the prey they are seeking to devour. If that were the case then they would never gain sufficient calories to replace the energy expended and thus they would never grow and mature.

Just because they will take a bunker chunk from the guy fishing next to you while ignoring your lure, does not make them lazy. Smart, wary of wooden or plastic objects with hooks, battle scarred, maybe. But I would not call them lazy. These majestic creatures are capable of short but explosive bursts of speed that give them the ability to ambush, and capture their prey. In fact, I don't think there are too many baitfish that could evade a large striper for long if the cow was intent on eating. What we do know is that large bass do not partake in feeding fests with their younger siblings with regularity. Are they in the area but in a neutral or non-feeding mood? We will probably never get a clear answer to this question. What we do know is that they like to feed on large meals. This fact is obviously derived from the large baitfish and lobsters that are often found in their stomachs. The natural conclusion is that large baitfish are much more filling than many small ones, and this requires fewer feeding times per day. This brings me back to slack, and changing water periods. During times of slack and changing water, a type of "shifting" takes place under the surface. Small stripers, which have been actively feeding on smaller baitfish funneled by current usually disperse. Steady action gives way to an occasional bump, but most surfcasters usually elect to take a break during this period. They grab a cup of coffee, change their lures, or they rest their casting shoulders, waiting for the current to reverse itself.

We were taught to think "moving water = good fishing" and this saying is for the most part correct. The flushing effect of strong current, which funnels the bait, coupled with dropping water levels, leaves baitfish fewer places to hide. Often this is the most productive tide period in back bays and inlet mouths. But if we are going to give large stripers credit for being smarter and more wary of striking strange objects like lures, are we also not going to question why will these extremely powerful and fast predators waste their energy during periods of fast moving water in order to feed? Everything in the surf is dependent on available food supply, always was and always will be. If the primary baitfish on which stripers are feeding are only present during the time when current is at its peak, then darn it, the cow stripers will be there too. But I share an opinion that these trophy stripers prefer to feed around slower water periods much more than during the faster ones. Remember, we are not talking about all stripers, only those brutes that keep reappearing in your dreams.

I mentioned shifting that takes place on the ocean bottom during a slack current period. Baitfish that were funneled and concentrated by current disperse and are no longer an attractive target to stripers. You would assume the stripers would take a break, and wait for current to once again help them in gathering and funneling baitfish. Actually, they do, but the biggest ones are often not part of this routine. It's important to remember that according to skin divers and scientists, truly big stripers tend to move

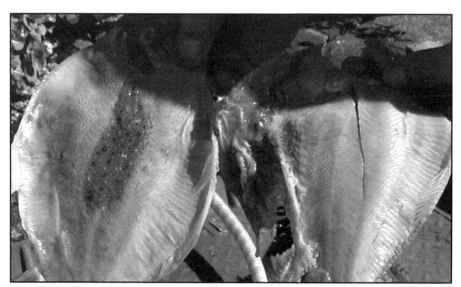

These two large fluke were only partially digested yet that did not stop a large striper from engulfing a bunker head.

in pods. Their feeding habits are not correlated with most of their younger siblings. They tend to feed infrequently, but on larger meals. During slack current periods, particularly in places where the current can run strong, at its peak, a game of musical chairs takes place during the period of slowing current. Large predatory fish like summer flounder will unearth themselves from their hiding places under the sand. Anticipating the change in current direction, they will attempt to position themselves with their heads facing the current. This way, once the current starts running, the food is going to be brought to them. But leaving their hiding place, camouflaged, and buried in the sand has its risk. Big stripers will often move in the shallow water during this period in order to feast on the summer flounder. In addition, it is not just the summer flounder that are attempting to change their position undetected. Winter flounder will act in a similar manner, especially in late spring when they gather on the backsides of the inlets, readying for their migration to cooler waters. Sea bass and blackfish are another item very high on the striped bass wish list. These two species will stay close to the rocks during the time of fast currents, but will leave their protective crevices during slower current periods to feed. This puts them in danger as large stripers cruise around rock piles, jetties and sandbars looking to gobble up any or all of these species. Remember, just one of these fish, be that blackfish, scup, sea bass or flounder will make a fine meal for a large striper, and will probably be all she will eat that day. If you still need convincing, I have a little story to tell you.

Slow moving current and change of current direction are disliked by many surfcasters, but they shouldn't be. Big fish often make forays into shallow water looking for one big meal.

Recently I fished with one of the contributing writers in this book. This particular night we fished a few places with nothing to show for our efforts. A hard west wind made back bay waters look like chocolate milk. We drove from place to place throwing lures and bait but found no one willing to play. We drove around for a long time looking to snag some fresh bunker, but found only three. This was in a place where thousands of bunker had beached themselves and died the previous day, trying to escape schools of marauding bluefish. We tossed our bunker snags, while at the same time holding our noses, trying to block out the putrid smell of decomposing bunker. After snagging our three lonely bunker, we ended up in the local inlet in the wee morning hours. There was about an hour left of ebb current and two guys were plugging hard, twenty yards in front of where we wanted to fish. The strong rip that was clearly evident earlier in the tide, had now started to dissipate. We sat in the truck and waited, fully dressed. The two guys passed by our truck and I got out, pretending to take my gear off. Sensing that I was leaving, and that they won't be giving anything away by talking to a guy who is also ready to pack it in, they told me that they had a few fish earlier in the tide. However, since the current slacked off, they had not gotten a bump for about an hour and a half. I told them we were running around the island most of the night with nothing to show for it.

You can sense when other surfcasters are enjoying your misery. Don't get me wrong, this is not a malicious kind of thing, but for some reason a surfcaster always gets his spirits up when you tell him you did worst than he did. We watched the guys take off their gear, and drive away while we deliberately fiddled with out gear, pretending we were packing too. As soon as their brake lights disappeared behind the dunes, we grabbed our conventional rods, which were hidden inside of our truck, and those three lonely bunker. We then walked to the exact spot these guys were standing on. We both impaled a bunker head on our hooks, along with a generous portion of the meat and cast it into the water. Within minutes, both of us were hooked up. Although these certainly were not monsters, they weren't schoolies either. The smallest fish was about twenty-four pounds. Within half an hour the current reversed direction and the bite came abruptly to a halt. The guys that left that night thought that bite had died along with the current, but on most nights that is not so.

Plugging slack water with live or rigged eels is an extremely productive strategy. Few surfcasters employ this technique. Tossing a fresh chunk during the same time is an equally productive approach. Try it! You might be pleasantly surprised.

DAY VERSUS NIGHT

Most surfcasters who have logged a few years in the suds know that fishing at night will give them the best chance of hooking up with a trophy striper. Is fishing at night that much better? Should you forsake sleep, and strictly concentrate your efforts on the hours between dusk and dawn? Yes and no. Big fish do make occasional forays into the surf zone under sunny skies, but those are rare events for specific reasons. What I mean by specific, is you can generally make pretty accurate assessments of why a herd of large cows are frolicking in the midday sun. At night the clues are a lot less obvious. Besides, big fish come to feed in the surf mostly at night so defining why they are there is much harder. In the daytime, they might be herding a school of bunker and pinning them against the beach, consequently coming within the reach of our cast.

New Jersey surfcasters have been the recipients of these spring daytime blitzes over the last few years. There is not much rhyme, or reason as far as the timing of these occurrences. It might happen at any point during the day. Large schools of big stripers, pushing adult bunker onto the beach is a sight every surfcaster should see at least once in their lifetime. Cape Cod Canal rats anticipate with glee a run of post migrating stripers as they make their ways through the Canal, usually feasting on herring or mackerel.

In addition, who hasn't heard about the wild action a Nor'easter can induce, as large stripers glide gracefully through large waves in search of disoriented baitfish and broken clams. As you can see, the presence of large bass in the surf during daylight hours is not uncommon, but these appearances are unpredictable and usually short in duration. Once the storm abates or the baitfish disperse, action will come to a halt almost instantaneously. Large stripers, faced with the lack of a big concentration of big baitfish, or having lost the big edge that rough water provides them, will retreat into the deeper water during the daytime.

For most of the year, (and when I say most, in some places this is 99%

Fishing at dusk is more convenient for fisherman but it is not the optimal time to target large stripers. If you are looking to tangle with big cows, stick to dawn and the hours of darkness.

while in others it might be closer to 90%) the surf zone is a barren sea in the daytime, at least when talking about large stripers. Yes, the action for a few weeks in the fall can be quite good, and some quality fish will be landed during daytime hours for sure. Yet, the night holds the key to consistency when it comes to hooking up with a large fish.

Occasionally, when conditions are right, a good bite will develop at dawn, usually on pencil poppers and metal lip swimmers. I am not certain exactly why dawn can be such a productive time period in the surf. Not much scientific research has been done on this subject, so we are left to our own suspicions. Is it because predators such as bass and bluefish feel an urgency to feed during low light levels? Is it that they know that they will soon have to retreat into deep water as light levels increase? Maybe the baitfish that have sought safety in numbers and had spent the nighttime hours concentrated in the shallow water must retreat into deeper water? Perhaps it is because baitfish cannot remain in shallow water otherwise they become susceptible to attacks by seagulls and other birds. Many baitfish will gather in the surf zone at night, seeking refuge from open waters where predators roam. But you'll rarely find them there during daylight hours. You might ask "What about dusk. Doesn't the setting sun present similar low light conditions as dawn does?" Yes, and predators do become more active but in my opinion, dusk is highly overrated, especially when compared to dawn. They might share similar characteristic in regard to light levels but they are not nearly as similar as they seem at first glance.

Dawn is the time when you generally will find more placid waters. The wind will usually be calmer than during the rest of the day. The baitfish that have gathered close to shore must seek deeper water, and stripers that patrol the outer edges of the sandbar will move toward the beach in hopes of intercepting the moving baitfish. The bite is usually more intense, as both baitfish and predators are usually gone by the time the sun is over the eastern horizon. Dawn is the time of tranquility, when most of the world is still asleep, boats are safely tied to the docks and the level of human activity is at a minimum. The only sound you will encounter is the screeching of seagulls looking for their morning meal. At dusk, the urgency to feed is just not there. What's the rush? They have all night to feed under the cover of darkness.

Often the tide will influence when the fish will be feeding more than the time of day.

Dusk on the other hand usually features increased noise levels, higher winds, swimmers still frolicking in the water and boats competing with us for prime beach real estate. Why is dusk then so popular in terms of anglers participation? I think the answer lies in convenience. Not many among us can be on the beach at dawn and make it into work on time. Dusk becomes a second best option for many surfcasters. It is far easier for many of us to go fishing after work than to go before work.

TIDE CONSIDERATION

I should mention that dawn (or any period during night or day) itself is not the event maker. You will still need a good tide to coincide with dawn. How do you find a good tide on the beaches you frequent? There is only one way and it's the most difficult one, but this sport in itself is very complicated. That is what makes it so special and challenging. The only way to find what the good time for a particular location might be is to fish this spot under different wind conditions and different stages of the tide, while keeping track of successes and failures in your logbook. Eventually, your logged entries will give you clues as to what stage of the tide, coupled with wind from a particular direction is the most productive. Although dawn might be a magical time to fish, and the scenery is often breathtaking, with rosy eastern skies and tranquility all around you, you might find yourself there at the wrong tide. Thus, you will probably accomplish nothing more than getting some good exercise. Just remember, a lousy tide, regardless of which time of day or night it occurs, is still a lousy tide. Take into the account that these early morning feeding patterns are short in duration. If you open your eyes and you see sunshine peeking through your bedroom window, you are probably too late. I prefer to be in the water, in the darkness, waiting for dawn to arrive. I have overslept many times only to gun my truck on the parkway and then hurriedly rush to the water, only to see my friends walking off the beach because the action had already died, and it wasn't even 6 A.M. yet!

I almost feel that I am trying to talk you into fishing during the daytime but trust me, I am not. The daytime action is usually confined to a very limited geographic area, and I feel you need to be able to do two things in order to cash in on these events. First, you need to be able to travel at the drop of a hat. An hour after a phone call during which you were informed about a great daytime bite at a particular location on two consecutive tides, should have you in your truck and on your way. This of course is difficult at best with family obligations. Do I ever feel jealous of those who make these runs freely because they are able to drop everything and go instantaneously while I always seem to have work and family obligations? Not for a moment. My wife and my kids were a gift from God himself, and there is no such animal, world record, or not, which would cause me to choose it over my responsibility as a father. My kids need a first base coach much more than I need another big fish, regardless of whether they win or lose.

Of course, when family life and that pesky thing called work ends up taking most of your time, you have a decision to make. Are you going to try to cash in on these occasional, daytime large fish blitzes, or are you going to target large fish at night exclusively? I find that I cannot do both. First, my daytime bag is full of different lures than my nighttime bag, my gear is different, and frankly I don't want to spend eight hours on the beach. So I choose to concentrate on the hours between dusk, and dawn, in my search for large stripers. Do you know what? I don't feel like I am missing out on anything. Of course, it doesn't hurt that more large fish are cruising in the surf at night than in the daytime.

As soon as the sun dips below the horizon, a transformation occurs in very shallow waters along our beaches. Baitfish tend to concentrate looking for safety in numbers. Predators like striped bass, weakfish, and bluefish feel empowered, and brazenly cruise in the same waters, where just an hour ago swimmers were frolicking.

If you are looking for a massive blitz at night, I hate to be the bearer of bad news, but this rarely ever happens. The feeding patterns at night are much more subdued, and done in a more "civilized" manner. Large stripers will take positions behind boulders, in the bridge shadows or they'll be cruising the lip of a sandbar, looking to ambush their prey. They will also nose into the jetties, and other rocky crevices looking for lobsters, crabs, and blackfish. That makes that pesky crab that's been steeling your bait on every cast much more important than that school of spearing joyfully playing around your waders. That crab might be tonight's dinner for a cow bass, and in turn attract the striper to your bait. I can almost guarantee that those spearing will not see the inside of a big striper's stomach.

Have you ever wondered, why these large bass are rarely ever in the surf and actively feeding during the day? When and where do they feed? Do they feed at night or only in deep water? I think there is a little bit of truth in both of these scenarios. Targeting large stripers in daytime is much more productive from a boat, than from the surf. Accept it, embrace it and learn to live with it. There are plenty of opportunities for a surfcaster to tangle with big bass, just not during the day. If you want consistency in your landings of large stripers, if you want to see the size of the fish you are catching increase, or if you want to give yourself the best possible chance to hook a fish of your dreams, fish at night.

I implore you to heed the advice of the extraordinary successful surfcasters who have done it time and time again over the years. Their success is a result of hard work, carefully kept logs and attention to details. But they all target large fish exclusively during nighttime hours. Their strategies and techniques might range from bait fishing to lures, or eels, but all these extremely successful big bass hunters all share one common thing. They target trophy stripers almost exclusively at night, and so should you.

CHAPTER FOUR

WATER CONDITIONS

While reading this book you might come to the realization that there is no single strategy for targeting large stripers. In fact, there are some conflicting opinions expressed among the contributing authors as to what kind of conditions they prefer when targeting big fish. "Conflicting" might be the wrong term to use, because truthfully, there is no one defined set of conditions that can be counted on to provide you with a shot at large stripers. Not on a regular basis at least.

Many of you who have read my book, "The Art of Surfcasting with Lures," are well aware that I am a "white water" nut. However when I choose to target large fish with eel skin plugs, I go out of my way to fish these lures in less turbulent waters. Before you start thinking that my obsession for fishing white water with lures has abated, let me put your mind at ease. White water will always be a big influence on how and when I fish the oceanfront beaches. Throwing my lure into the white, foamy water that a collapsing wave leaves behind is something I daydream about. But it's just not what I do when I am hunting for a trophy striper with an eel skin plug. Rigged with a skin, these lures tend to get tossed around in turbulence, and more often than not, the tail ends up wrapped around the treble hook. It is also difficult to present an eel skin plug in rough surf in a manner that would imitate the eel's snakelike motion. Besides, white water does such a good job of "masking" our lure for a few moments, that using an eel skin lure is actually counterproductive. For this reason, I tend to concentrate my efforts in areas with less turbulence and calmer water when using eel skin plugs, such as on inlet jetties, alongside the back bay bridges, and on the backsides of inlets.

Do I feel the areas that I target hold bigger fish, or do I fish there because my eel skin lures are more productive there? The answer is a little bit of both. One of the keys to catching a big fish regardless of the location, or the structure you are targeting is to use a lure (or bait) that you can present in the most natural manner possible.

CALM OR ROUGH WATER?

When it comes to choosing the right water conditions to target big bass, the choice is not as obvious as the one detailed above. In my humble opinion,

Big fish cruise the calm, shallow waters more often then you think.

you have a better chance of hooking up with the fish of your dreams under calm to moderate conditions, than you do under rough surf conditions. Before many of you start rolling your eyes at me, allow me to explain. I am a big believer that large fish are present in the areas we fish more often than we think. After all, there is no "old ladies club" in the ocean where these big girls go during the day to play cards. Even when not actively feeding, they are constantly on the move, and since they do most of their feeding in shallow waters, we can assume that large fish are lurking in the areas we fish more often then we would like to admit. You might ask why we don't hook them more often. Would a bass of any size, be able to resist a nice lure wiggling in front of its face? My answer is absolutely, positively, yes. I've seen it, and experienced it enough times. My opinion about the presence of big fish in the surf at any given time has changed dramatically over the last few years. I've often seen live or rigged eels entice a cow, while everyone was catching small fish on lures.

In June 2008, I took a trip to Cuttyhunk, MA with my buddy Tommy

Corrigan. He did extensive artwork on my previous book and I wanted to show my appreciation by taking him with me. Besides, he is a hell of a surfcaster, with the stamina of a bull and a wicked sense of humor. I certainly did not have to worry about being bored on this trip, as Tommy made the ride from New York to New Bedford, MA pass quickly with his wisecracks. The reports that I had obtained from Cuttyhunk were not very promising. Granted, not too many people were fishing there, so reports were scarce, but the ones we did get pointed to inconsistent fishing and mostly school bass. In fact, one of the contributing writers, Manny Moreno, was there a few days before we arrived. He did better than most of the other fishermen, with some fish in the 20's, but not nearly as well as he expected. What was even more disconcerting was that his fishing partner, a well-seasoned surfcaster in his own right, went fishless for the whole trip. Manny, whom I hold in high regard, is considered one of the best and most aggressive surfcasters of my generation. I thought that if he did not do well, what were my chances? I did not mention this to Tommy as we boarded the ferry to Cuttyhunk. I did not want to lower his hopes and enthusiasm, which is contagious.

After an hour-long ride on the ferry, we arrived in Cuttyhunk harbor. We checked into the Cuttyhunk Striped Bass Club, and shortly afterwards we took a stroll to Southwest Point. It was just a leisurely stroll to get Tommy familiar with the area we would fish that night. Upon returning to the Striped Bass Club, Tommy took off his shoes, and showed me two large blisters, one on the back of each foot. He taped them heavily before putting on his wetsuit, and his Korkers boots. We both wore wetsuits for the duration of the trip. I had fished Cuttyhunk a few times in waders and I'd done OK, but I wanted to fish from some of the massive rocks that were a little further from the shore. By the time our trip was over, I swore I would never return there without a wetsuit. Another thing I'll never return without is a rigged eel, but first things first.

We started fishing the first night in front of the Striped Bass Club. There were a bunch of big boulders that resembled a broken up jetty, but in actuality, they were the remains of an old "bass stand". Many years ago, very affluent people would stand on these stands that were built out of wood, and placed on top of these boulders. They would have a servant with them, who would bait their hooks with lobster tails, and cast their

Wetsuits have made it possible for surfcasters to reach deep water, whenever conditions allow.

lines into the surf. Today, a column of rocks is all that remains in the water.

I waded to the lead rock, while Tommy got onto a big boulder about 30 yards away. He drew first blood by nailing a 22-pound bass on a Super Strike Darter. For the next hour we had a pretty consistent pick of fish on darters, and needlefish, but they were all less than 10 pounds. After awhile, the action slowed down to an occasional bump and neither one of us hooked up or landed a fish for almost an hour. I yelled over to Tommy to ask if he was ready to move on to the next spot. I wanted to cover as much ground as possible. This way, if we found fish to be stacked up in any particular location, we could concentrate our efforts there in the next few nights. He asked if he could make a few more casts and I obliged.

After removing a needlefish from my snap, I attached a rigged eel. I've been on a sporadic rigged eel kick, on and off for years. I use them enough to know what I am doing, but not enough in order to acquire the confidence I sorely need. After reading Manny's chapter on rigged eels while putting this book together, and speaking to Manny on the phone, before the trip, I got re-excited about using them. Manny fishes rigged eels almost exclusively when conditions allow, and after learning this, I was intrigued. I decided then on this trip, I would give them at least an honest effort, if nothing else. I leaned into my rod, and cast a rigged eel toward the light that was coming from Martha's Vineyard. I started to retrieve the eel with a rhythmic motion, by lowering my tip, and raising it, and then repeating the process while cranking the reel. My eel was stopped dead in its track, and my rod doubled over. The drag, which I loosened up while we were catching smaller fish, was singing and line was peeling in an alarming fashion. I tightened up on the drag and fought the fish for a few minutes before sliding it on a large boulder where I was standing. I turned on my light only to hear Tommy yell, "Nice fish". A quick measurement on a Boga scale registered 24 pounds and then quickly back into the water it went. Two casts later I got walloped again and this fish was almost identical in size to the last one. As soon as I hooked into a second fish, I yelled to Tommy, "Put on a rigged eel!" He wasn't getting any hits on lures now for more than an hour. He switched to a rigged eel, and made a cast. His rigged eel landed in the water with a big "plop" and while the ripples of water from where his eel landed were still evident on the surface, I heard him yell, "I'm in!" Moments latter Tommy put his Boga on a fish that ended up being our best fish of the night, just shy of 30 pounds.

You might say that those fish just arrived in the area and we got lucky. You might be right, but I don't think so. I think they were there and wanted no part of eating our lures. How can I be so certain? You can never be a hundred percent sure, but when it happens often enough, you start to believe it and on this particular trip it happened wherever we went.

The next day we scouted a cove on the south side of the island and decided to fish it that night. When we first arrived we caught small bass on about every lure we threw. They were feeding less than 30 yards in front of us, which made Danny swimmers very effective. Unfortunately, due to an open snap, I lost my "mojo" Beachmaster Danny. You know the one that I always carry which has enticed more strikes than all the lures in my bag combined? Yes, that old warrior was last seen floating somewhere on the south side of Cuttyhunk. If you find it, treat it with care, I would bet it still has a lot of fish catching ability left. To lose a great plug to a fish is admirable, but to lose it because I did not properly closed the snap is embarrassing, and quite upsetting.

The night before, I had lugged a massive Hunter bag around my neck. The darn thing acted like an anchor around my neck when I tried to get up onto the rocks. As a result I decided to switch to a single row Aquaskinz bag. This bag has fewer lure tubes than the Hunter bag so I had to leave some of the plugs back at the Club. I looked through the bag for another Danny swimmer but I knew that was the only one I had with me. I just had a few needlefish and darters.

Considering most of the fish we caught were small, it seemed silly to throw a rigged eel, but then again, sometimes I just like doing silly stuff. Besides, I was hoping to cull a better fish out of this school. I thought about how we banged good size fish under the Club on rigged eels, the night before, yet those fish wanted no part of our lures. So I decided to throw a rigged eel, and to my surprise I was rewarded on my first cast with a high teen bass, followed up by a few fish in the mid-twenties. Tommy immediately switched to a rigged eel, and the fish he was catching now also got bigger.

Still not convinced? The next night we ended up on the island's western most point. I had to bob in the water for the last 20 yards to get onto the rock I wanted. This rock was massive in size but a pain in the ass to get on top. It was shaped like a diamond, with a big, flat plateau above water level but nothing underneath. I was swimming around it, trying to stick my feet into the rock's crevices to push myself on top, but I wasn't very successful. I took my rod and placed it on the top of a rock. While still

Getting on a top of a distant rock can be a very unpleasant experience, particularly at night. Take safety into consideration before wading into the water.

bobbing in the water, I removed my Aquaskinz bag and also placed it onto the rock. This gave me two free hands to use to climb onto this sucker. Of course, one large wave, and my rod and bag would be swept into a dark abyss of bubble weed and boulders. I had to get on top of this rock before a swell arrived. Digging my fingernails into the slimy moss, I somehow pushed myself onto the rock, and then inched upwards over the rock on my belly like a seal. My feet were still dangling too far under the rock in order push myself up onto it. Suddenly, the water level behind me dropped, almost instantaneously. I knew what this meant from fishing Montauk rocks. For every action there is an equal and opposite reaction and this was no exception as a big swell was about to hit me. I quickly grabbed my rod with one hand, and my bag with the other, while still lying on my belly. As I felt the surge coming close I tried to elevate my dangling feet. I knew that if I didn't, the swell would slam me into the rock and I'd probably slide off the rock again. I was right! By elevating my legs I was pushed over the big boulder. I managed to stand up before the next swell arrived, and got ready to fish.

The first few casts with lures went untouched. I knew we were going to lose the tide soon, so I decided not to play with lures, but instead attached a rigged eel to my leader. On the next six consecutive casts I caught quality fish, each one weighing more than 22 pounds. On the seventh cast I hooked into something that resembled a train more than a fish. The line was peeling off the reel while I struggled to hold on. After a lengthy battle, I brought the fish to within 10 yards of the rock I was standing on. I knew she would probably make one more run for freedom and I was right. Sensing shallow water, or maybe the rock I stood on, she took off, which was fine as I was fully prepared for it. What I did not expect was that the drag on my Van Staal would seize. I was yanked off the rock, and head first into the water. When I resurfaced and reeled the line back, I found a broken 80-pound leader. I got back onto the rock a little easier now, as the tide was higher, and let out a scream that was probably heard on Block Island. That was the last rigged eel I had on me, the rest of them were stored in Ziploc bags in my backpack on the shore. I tied a new leader, and started casting darters, and needlefish. The only thing I caught was a three-pound bass on an eel skin needlefish.

After about half an hour of fruitless exercise, I jumped into the water,

Rigged eels catch big fish almost all the time but you'll need the right conditions to use them effectively.

and bobbed back to shore. After grabbing three more rigged eels from my backpack, I scrambled to get back on the rock before the tide had slacked off. Would you believe it if I told you, that on the first cast with a fresh rigged eel I had a 26-pound bass? Then another fish in the high 20's and then disaster struck again. I brought the fish, which was in the 40-pound range, close to the rock, maybe a rod length away. My drag was working flawlessly and when she made a last ditch attempt for deep water, I wasn't going to let her yank me off the rock again, even if my drag seized again. Unfortunately, that is exactly what happened, me standing on a ten-foot wide boulder, and her going for deep water. I held on to the rod, and for a moment I actually thought that I had a shot, seized drag and all, when a loud piercing "pop" of snapped leader echoed through the darkness. I do not know why the leader gave out but I have been told that when reeling in line under very little tension, the braid buries itself into the spool when a fish hits. This can cause your leader to give. Whatever the reason, it was a night I'll never forget and I will not visit Cuttyhunk again without a wetsuit or rigged eels.

You might ask "What the hell does this have to do with rough/calm water conditions for big bass?" Everything! If the wind were any higher, I could not use the rigged eels in the manner that I described. Plus I think you'll agree with me that I was successful with my eels not because of my skill but because the fish were there and they wanted rigged eels. If the water were rougher, I probably could not get on that rock and fish the deep water that was around it. This is why I prefer calmer water when targeting big bass. It gives me more options with regard to what lures I can use.

Many years ago I asked Manny, "What is the best time to use live eels on Montauk's south side"? He could have BS'd me and gave me "new moon/dropping tide/southwest wind" mumbo jumbo, but he didn't. He summed it up in three simple words, "When you can." What I assume he meant was to throw them whenever conditions allow. Guess what? You can't throw live eels in a rough surf or a strong head wind. You can't throw rigged ones either or at least not that effectively. In addition, needlefish and eel skin plugs will not win any prizes either under those conditions. This is why I say that I prefer the calmer conditions much more than rough ones. More strategies that are known to be effective can be employed and more weapons can be used.

FISHING BIG WATER

Hunting for big stripers in big water conditions has its fans. Just because I like certain conditions, that doesn't mean that everyone will. This is why

Casting into rough surf can be productive but not nearly as productive as working the night tides.

I said in the beginning the "one size fits all" answer has no place in the surf. Nothing will get Montauk regulars more excited than a Nor'easter barreling up the coast. Huge swells and sheets of rain that are horizontally driven by the wind and white water galore are not everyone's cup of tea. However, I certainly enjoy fishing under those conditions. Thankfully, this is mostly a daytime affair. Trying to mount a rock in the middle of the night is best left to those with experience, strong stamina, and a high tolerance for pain. If you have heard about the great action a Nor'easter can inspire at Montauk Point, but are not exactly sure why this happens, take a look at a map. The Montauk Point Lighthouse faces east. As the incoming tide rolls in from the ocean, it goes around the lighthouse and heads northwest. At the same time, a strong Northeast blow will push everything diagonally onto the beach. With these two factors converging, any baitfish that happen to be in the water at this time will find themselves pushed towards the shoreline in what is best described as washing machine like turbulence. However, the baitfish are no match for this type of water. They are tossed about and become disoriented and are easy prey for stripers that cruise effortlessly through these big swells and white water. If the bait in the surf is plentiful and of the large variety, you can expect a banner day, with large stripers moving into the surf from deep water rips.

Due to the high winds and high surf conditions, you will be limited to the lures you can use. Most seasoned surfcasters will grab a handful of bucktails and pork rinds, and leave their surf bags in their trucks. Bucktails are about the only lure you can effectively use under these conditions with the exception of tins. At night, a bottle plug becomes a very useful tool, especially on sandy beaches. High surf associated with these storms will usually unearth thousands of clams from the bottom. They will be tossed about, and in the process many of them will crack open. This in turn will create a natural chum slick that will bring stripers into the surf zone, even if there is no other bait present. In my opinion, this is one of the rare occurrences where bait is not a prerequisite for the appearance of big fish in the surf. Many claim that after the storm has abated your chances of catching a quality fish will rise because the big, opportunistic stripers will be gobbling clams in the wash. I do agree with this general statement, but I think catching these fish is more difficult than it is under normal or calmer conditions.

Even after the winds have calmed down, rough surf conditions can persist for days. Couple that with incredible numbers of broken clams in the surf and dirty water and you can see why this strategy is not always that productive. One or two big fish are caught by those who toss clams, or tins, but for the most part, very few fish are caught compared to the number of surfcasters who fish these storm leftovers.

Nor'easters are not the only storm systems that can produce a good bite with quality fish. Strong northwest winds, late in the year can produce banner days for those present on the beach. Northwesterly winds usually produce small, choppy surf instead of big swells and it is a lot easier to fish during the night.

Again, the key in my opinion is the location where you will be fishing and how the wind direction correlates with where you are standing. I find that an ideal situation is a northwest wind that comes at you diagonally together with a current that is moving in the same direction. With the wind blowing in the same direction as the tide is moving, the current increases in speed and the baitfish are pushed onto the beach. Bucktails, bottle plugs and darters can be deadly under these conditions. Of course, all these rough conditions won't help you one bit if there is no bait in the area.

What you prefer, as a big fish hunter, is to have any of these wind conditions coincide with the presence of large baitfish in the surf zone. Juvenile weakfish, bunker, herring or mullet, will bring much bigger bass into the surf than sand eels, spearing or peanut bunker.

In late September, look for mullet to leave the confines of the inlets and head westward along our shore beaches. I prefer strong southwesterly winds to create ample white water feeding opportunities for stripers. Again, if you are looking for that fish of a lifetime, these are usually not prime conditions. As mullet are large bait, you can expect to catch many quality fish, but I find that the big brutes will rarely join in the feeding frenzy under a midday sun. Once the sun sets in the west and darkness engulfs the shoreline bunker chunks will produce more cows even though the stripers are actively feeding on mullet. You can count on daytime commotion, especially if bluefish are in on the action, in their marauding ways, to draw large stripers in the surf at night to look for leftovers.

Yes, I know it's maddening that truly trophy stripers rarely partake in these daytime blitzes; even when large bait like mullet is in the wash. In my personal experience, you can expect the size of the fish to be larger, just not jumbo size. I also know that it is frustrating to be a plugger who walks the beaches in search of that elusive cow. You can do everything right. Get up at the crack of dawn, after the first strong cold front in September, you can find mullet, and you may also find an area where stripers and blues can coral bait for a prolonged period of time. Then you have the time of your life bailing nice sized stripers and blues all day. However, after you get up the next morning, hoping for the action to repeat itself, you find out that during the night the action featured only a few fish, but they were trophy size specimens.

I don't believe you can be a successful trophy hunter by only using artificial lures. I think it's commendable that some stick with them, even when the bite has switched from lures to bait. Many lure purists will be successful in their endeavors if they live in areas that generally feature more big fish than many others like Montauk Point or Block Island. But I still think that fishermen whose main goal is to catch big fish and then worry about how they did it later, will have a better rate of success. I am convinced that large stripers will take a rigged eel, live eel, or bait most of the time without giving it a second thought while at the same time ignoring lures. Even eel skin lures that I love so much will take

Fooling a big striper with a lure is difficult but certainly not impossible.

a backseat to these three heavyweights. Catching a trophy striper on a lure is in my view the most difficult accomplishment for a surfcaster but then this is what makes it so rewarding. To know that you fooled, hooked and landed a giant striper on a piece of wood, plastic or metal is the ultimate dream of many surfcasters.

I am confident that the advice in the upcoming chapters from some of the most successful big fish hunters today will help you greatly in achieving your goal of catching larger fish, more often. Doc Muller will eloquently fill you in on the current state of surfcasting in an upcoming chapter, while Jimmy D'Amico will present strategies for getting out on the rocks where the big girls often lie. His views on gear go beyond the advice you might have received in the past. His mission is to make you aware of all the things you might consider before you embark on your mission of catching a cow striper.

In Part Two of the book you will find specific strategies and techniques for targeting and catching large stripers. Written by Alberto Knie, John Skinner, Steve McKenna, Bill Wetzel and Manny Moreno, these chapters will open the window into the minds of these very successful surfcasters. I am confident that by following their advice you will catch more and bigger fish in the future.

Please remember that no advice in this book should be taken as gospel and you should never attempt to push yourself beyond your comfort zone and into a possible life threatening situation. No fish is worth your life, regardless of its size. We all have wives, kids and families to come home to regardless of how many fish we catch. Stay safe and look out for others who might not know the dangers that await them under the surface.

CHAPTER FIVE

THE IMPORTANCE OF GEAR
By Jimmy D'Amico

As an avid fisherman and hands on fabricator I'd like to share my thoughts on something that's quite often last on most surfcasters "to do list"; *outfitting yourself with the right personal gear.* Now... if there were a defined line in this category between right and wrong, covering this topic would be much simpler. Instead, this decision should ultimately be left for each individual surfcaster to make on a case-by-case basis. Naturally, like any other sport and as reflected on many of today's Internet talk sites, opinions will vary greatly, but choices should always be made wisely. Because it's no secret that our odds for catching trophy bass often increase when fishing some considerably difficult (sometimes dangerous) locations under the dark of night, fumbling with gear is absolutely not an option. What I'd like for you to walk away with after reading this chapter is not only an increased awareness regarding the use of certain surfcasting gear, but more importantly a strategic thought process that can be applied to your favorite location and style of fishing when preparing to adapt and overcome the unforgiving elements. Having fished a wide variety of surf environments, the location I mainly prefer is Montauk Point, NY. In my opinion, Montauk is one of the most diverse locations to fish in the northeast and is extremely taxing on one's body and personal gear. For me, this just adds to the overall challenge because having the right gear at Montauk can sometimes mean the difference between catching schoolie or cow bass. I say "sometimes" because there's always the chance of catching a 50 in the middle of the day on a bunker chunk thrown 10-yards from the shoreline by someone using a conventional boat outfit. Where the "right gear" comes into play is when consistency is your objective.

Before attempting to start you off in the right direction I would like to set some discussion parameters. First, there are many different brand names of gear to choose from today. Which name brand you ultimately choose is a matter of personal preference. Second, it would be nearly impossible for me to cross-reference each and every type of surfcasting environment as they relate to personal gear (i.e. – bridges, jetties, open sand beaches, inlets, sandbars, offshore rocks and free swimming); however, what I cover should be applicable to several of these areas. Third, for the most part my examples will revolve around what I know best, that being wading the rips or swimming to outer rocks in Montauk; AKA wetsuiting. Therefore, I would like to point out that what has "worked" for me throughout the years may very well not work for you, however, I do suggest applying my same level of thought towards your own specific style of fishing. Last, equally important as having the right gear will be how it's configured on your person. In other words, you'll soon learn through trial and error that what sometimes appears as being the perfect gear setup (pre-trip) may actually end up requiring numerous post-trip adjustments or modifications in order to be most effective (i.e. – the ability to easily re-secure gear is just as important as easily accessing it in the first place). That said; let's get down to business...

PERSONAL WEAR

The foundation of most surfcasters' gear (personal wear) arsenal almost always begins with a set of chest waders and a rain top. Although I frequently avoid making the "cost factor" a "deciding factor", as I've always felt that it was the least important issue when purchasing the right gear or wear for the sport I love, this category would be an exception to my rule. As you graduate from fishing areas that are easily reachable from where you have parked to traversing remote locations for long distances in such places as Montauk's "south side", I can assure you that you'll get what you pay for. In other words, that fifty dollar set of rubber waders may keep you dry as a bone from the outside in, but it's your body perspiration that will have you wishing you went the extra "yard" for those breathable waders you've read about. Next, that rain jacket you may have bought because it would offer ample protection should the skies open up may also have worked well against the splash rising off the waters edge, however, I can assure you that a long walk over rocky terrain will have you feeling that the cost for a quality breathable dry or semi-dri top was money well spent. My best advice for you in this category is to do extensive research prior to purchase and don't be afraid to "think out of the box". In other words, there are very few wader or dry top manufacturers who will target the captive surfcasting audience. Those who do generally understand our needs by offering products constructed of lightweight, rugged and breathable materials, but your choices extend even further. Doing a simple search on the Internet for products targeting the kayak, river (fly fishing) or sailing communities will often be more than adequate with features that reach beyond the norm. Also be sure to look into products built for military applications. Quite often you will

Chest waders and rain top shield us not only from the rain but from winds and underwater hazards too.

find military contractors who are permitted to offer "over-run" products through one or two retailers. Basically, the name of the game in the wader/dry top category is to identify personal wear that will keep you dry and comfortable, yet be built rugged enough to withstand the type of environment you're fishing.

Rapidly growing in popularity since the mid-80's is the use of wetsuits to reach remote locations such as outer sandbars and rocks positioned in deep waters. After being proven effective by surfcasters who pioneered the idea, mainly for safety reasons, we're now able to fish zones that large bass frequent without fear of consequence should we be swept off our perch by strong currents or waves. This is not to say that we're invincible,

Today's surfcaster uses a wetsuit as a tool in order to fish safely and comfortably from the distant rocks and sandbars.

but rather that we now have an edge to reach trophy bass lying in certain spots that were reachable only by boat in years past. Just in time to coincide with Montauk's new "wetsuiting craze" is a new generation of suits that are seemingly better designed for surfcasters than divers. The reason I say this is that most wetsuit manufacturers have now introduced "stretchable" materials that give us the freedom of movement necessary to cast for hours on end without muscle fatigue. Although this new generation of neoprene works well for us, divers are claiming that material compression at depths beyond 90 feet can cause a rapid escape of body heat; hence, these new wetsuits may be more "suitable" for the surfcaster than the diver. When researching what suit you should buy, be sure to cross-reference the water temperatures you intend on fishing with the thickness of suit materials used (mfg's millimeter rating). Also for your consideration is whether to purchase a one or two-piece wetsuit. Personally, I prefer using a two-piece 3mm wetsuit during late Spring thru early Fall, then switching to a 7/5mm one-piece for the remainder of the year. My reasoning for this choice is that I can shed the top portion of the two-piece 3mm during warm summer nights if my intension is to wade a sandbar in chest high water or can wear both top and bottom for added buoyancy if I plan on swimming to an outer rock. Late Fall I choose to wear a 7/5 mm because water and air temps can rapidly drop overnight. Having a one-piece 7mm suit with 5mm sleeves simply allows more freedom of movement for casting and is a combined mm rating I highly recommend.

Last, but not least, in the personal wear department is the use of a dry suit. Still relatively low in popularity, this type of protection will just get an honorable mention. Within the three personal wear categories, finding the right dry suit for the job will require the most research of all on your behalf. Dry suits range from white water kayaking to military/rescue design and quality. If staying absolutely dry from the neck down is what you desire, my advice would be to shop for a suit without valves that's constructed of a highly durable/breathable outer shell; boot or stocking foot is a matter of preference. Also be sure to directly verify with the manufacturer whether or not they offer a gasket replacement service, what the approximate turnaround time is and what the estimated cost will be including shipping. As in the wader category, I mention the "cost factor" because a bargain dry suit may be priced that way for a reason… and not only because of the perspiration factor. Inexpensive dry suits usually equate to a tear prone outer shell. Remember, you're not going to be in a river during daylight hours. You will more than likely be fishing the edge of a very big ocean at night, one that may wisely motivate you to wear an inflatable PFD/dry suit combo. All in all, the trend of warmer late season water temperatures in Montauk since the mid 90's has changed surf migration patterns of large bass, therefore, putting a stalemate on the popularity growth of "dry suiting".

Straddling the line between personal wear and essential gear is footwear. Chances are that when pushing your limits to the edge of the envelope by venturing past the line of danger that most others wisely refrain from crossing, having the proper footwear will be of the utmost importance. Your two main areas of concern should be slippery rocks and soft or shifting sand. For planned preparedness in these areas, slight design modifications to "off the shelf" products may be necessary. For instance, when fishing under the Montauk Lighthouse, rocky shoreline or a jetty, most studded sandals will work fine straight out of the box. Wade out to a rock located 50-yards off the beach and they may not still be strapped to your boots once you get there. In the event they are, those

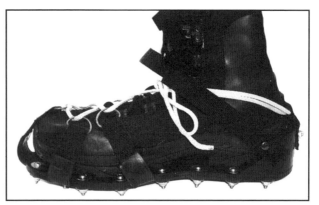

Korker modification by Jimmy D'Amico.

"replaceable studs" underneath may have helped themselves through a self-removal process by falling out along the way! Like anything else there are a number of ways to achieve the same end goal, which in this case should be to better secure the cleats to your boots and take the appropriate measures to prevent the studs from falling out. What I've found is that heel lift is the main culprit when it comes to cleat loss. In my opinion, the best remedy for this is to create a loop out of a 1 or 2 inch wide x 5 inch long piece of heavy polypropylene webbing, doubling it over (fold in ½) and bolting it straight thru the heel of the sandal. What you've now created is a much-needed loop at the heel for which to run the laces through; if longer laces are necessary, replacement may be required. Next, I would suggest addressing the possibility of missing studs by replacing them in full with stainless steel screws, fender washers and lock nuts. The screws may not give you as much "bite" as the carbide studs; however, they'll at least be there when you need them. Further sandal modifications may also include the addition of a few extra studs in the toe area for that occasional "second life" you may need on the rock in rough water, as well as protecting the stock strapping from abrasion by covering them with cut pieces of heater hose. On a much simpler note, preparation for wading soft or shifting sand in a wetsuit will be much more comfortable if you fold the very bottom of your suit over the top of your boots. Much like gravel guards work for stream fishermen, this will help prevent two pounds of sand from entering into each boot through the top.

ESSENTIAL GEAR

Before moving on to discuss some specific types of essential gear, I'd like to share my thoughts on the evolution of an essential component that anchors the gear to us; that being the wading belt. Years ago, the main reason why surfcasters wore wading belts was to cinch up the waist area in order to prevent water from seeping under one's rain top and into the waders; *causing a dangerous situation*. Back then; belts weren't utilized for much more than their intended purpose – plus, possibly to hold a plier sheath, gaff, stringer and knife. Because most fishermen in the early days primarily waded the shallow surf zone with light gear, the need for heavy-duty belts with strong quick detach buckles virtually did not exist. Now this isn't to say that rain or dry tops today don't need to be cinched around one's waist for safety reasons, but as we try to draw the line between what gear we want to carry and what gear we actually need to carry, the surf belt is where these items are most likely going to be affixed. As I've observed, this evolution is mirrored in our present day. What I mean by this is that most new surfcasters will (at first) still purchase the type of belt solely needed to keep the waist line cinched tight, as well as carry a few light pieces of gear. As they transition over time from casual to serious surfcaster targeting large bass, the need to carry additional specialized type gear increases. As they begin setting up one or more belts for use in certain specific areas, history is fast-forwarded from the requirements of the early surfcaster to those of modern day. Personally, as a "wetsuiter", the need to keep water out of my suit simply does not exist. What does exist is my need for a stiff belt that's constructed of materials rated to withstand countless trips in and out of a saltwater environment. The belt cannot bend, twist or sag in any way under a nominal gear load and must secure via a positive locking buckle designed to guard against accidental opening. Equally, if not more, important is the fact that the belt I personally choose must have the ability to be easily and quickly shed in the event I'm faced with a life-threatening situation. Remember, as we continue pushing the limits of where we go and how we fish, we must remain vigilant of safety. As a side note to choosing the proper wading belt, look for one with an average width of 2-inches, as most plug bags, accessory sheaths and pouches are designed with a belt loop having a 2 ¼" – 2 ½" opening. Also, if you intend on utilizing every inch of space

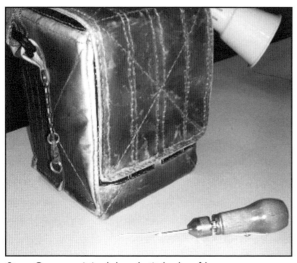

Steve Campo original, hand-stitched surf bag.

on it to slide or bolt gear to, a fairly reliable gauge to use when trying to determine whether the belt will be sufficient or not is "If you're able to fold it over flat numerous times, it's probably under-rated for your intended use."

The first major gear component that most every surfcaster today owns is a plug bag. Plug bags can be purchased anywhere from your favorite local tackle shop to most any major sporting goods retailer. Bag qualities range from absolute junk to high-end quality construction. Funny thing about the plug bag is that most of us couldn't imagine fishing without one, yet it's not that long ago that there were very few on the market. Proof of this lies in photos dating up to the mid-60's where you'll find surfcasters mainly using makeshift bags to carry their lures. It wasn't until around the mid 60's that a guy, who actually wasn't a fisherman, identified the need for a "retail plug bag" and began building them out of a basement shop, located in East Northport, Long Island. From what I've been told, his bags sold for approximately fifteen dollars through a few local tackle shops and were available until the late 70's before being discontinued. There are still a few of those bags around today, most of which have withstood the test of time by such hardcore fishermen as the guys from "Murderer's Row"... *False Bar, N.Y. of course.* I'm not sure if Jim Reid, builder of those early khaki colored canvas bags with riveted sheet metal inserts, was the guy who actually thought of placing numerous vertical compartments in a bag, but whoever it was definitely must have stayed up all night thinking of the idea!

During the late 70's an old school and extremely low-key fisherman named Steve Campo, who I personally regard as being the best to have ever fished Montauk and Block Island, began raising the bar in plug bag quality by handcrafting his own; *one stitch at a time.* His bags were constructed of water shedding sailcloth and sized to meet specific requirements based on intended location, time of year and method of use. Steve's combination of basic functional design, superior material choice and overall bulletproof construction not only proved to be highly effective in a wetsuit environment, but has earned his labor intense bags a place in surfcasting history as being, bar none, the absolute best to have ever been built.

All in all, unlike the early days, today there are many different brands of plug bags to choose from, some of which offer countless options such as pockets within pockets and other "bells and whistles". My best advice to you when deciding which bag will best suit your needs is to keep it simple and sized accordingly. Remember, targeting trophy bass from the surf usually means that you'll be covering some rough terrain in the dark of night under various adverse weather and surf conditions. What will work in your favor shall be a bag that's well organized and wisely filled with everything you "need to carry" not necessarily what you may "want

to take along just in case. "As a wetsuiter," time is of the essence" every time I need to access something inside of my bag. Fumbling around in the main storage compartment or one of the accessory pockets is not an option. My bag is like a well organized shop; I know where things are before reaching for them. Additional personal requirements worth sharing are that I

A quality bag is an essential component of any surfcaster's gear.

prefer a quick draining, full Velcro closure bag that's built with longevity in mind. Having an ample number of large grommets is an important factor after wading or swimming out to a rock that you must lift the weight of yourself and a water-filled bag up onto. Longevity or a lack thereof comes into play after your bag has been soaked then dried out numerous times. Choosing a bag with high-quality seam stitching intended to guard against dry rot and the pressure of water weight should help guard against the type of failure that (for many) seems to occur at the worst of times. Oh and unless you want to watch a school of colorful plugs float past you, I would like to reiterate the importance of choosing a bag with an ample amount of polyester Velcro holding the lid shut.

I'd now like to take a personal approach to what I term as "essential gear" by covering the what, why and how of items I use when wetsuiting. What I'm hoping you'll develop after I share this with you is not a list of items you should run out and buy, but a thought process by which you should determine what will work best for you in the environment you're fishing. Please keep in mind that although personal gear may be small in size, it's my opinion that when it comes to trophy bass fishing, each individual item is as equally important as the rod and reel you're using. After all, the name of the game is to cast, retrieve, hopefully hook and quickly release your fish so you can do it again; this will be a bit tough to do if you're busy fumbling with your gear.

I guess a fair approach to telling you what I do use is by also commenting on what I don't use. That sentence may seem a bit strange, at least it does to me, but when it comes to the "weight factor" I don't carry a scale or lip grip tool. I fully understand that surfcasting clubs compete in seasonal tournaments based on accurate bass weight; however, I don't partake in this type of competition and therefore resort to "guesstimation" based on my past experience with scales. As far as the lip grip tool, I think they are an awesome replacement to the gaffs that were swinging from almost every surfcaster's wading belt in Montauk years ago. Throughout all the years I carried a gaff it was only used once on a 44 that I hooked while "skishing" approximately 100+ yards off the beach. After the bass took me for quite a ride I was too exhausted to lift it out of the wash and decided to drag it out with the gaff hook. Other than that one time, my thumb has always served me well and will remain as my method of choice

Korkers, belts, Boga grip, leader wallets, pliers and flashlights are just some of the tools a surfcaster might need to assist in climbing on rocks or when landing or unhooking a fish.

in order to avoid carrying the extra added weight on my belt; *including the gaff I no longer carry.*

Starting from the neck down is something that's a must for night fishing; *a flashlight.* The light I carry is a high-end military grade LED flashlight that weighs only 2.2 ounces (with battery), is constructed of quality aircraft aluminum that will resist impact and has a watertight rating down to 10 feet; thanks to a double "O" ring seal. It is affixed to a 3/16" ID surgical tube neck lanyard for comfort and quick acquisition when needed with a tethered tail cap to guard against loss during a potential battery change while out on a rock. The light has four separate LED circuit boards, so I no longer carry a second light around my neck. I prefer LED technology for its reliability, clarity and available color choices. Today, most surfcasters utilize a red light when fishing in order to keep their activities stealth and maintain their night vision after the light is turned off. I personally prefer an NVIS (Night Vision Imaging System) light, which has a greenish hue, is as "low key" as the color red and generates a visible light that makes it easier to decipher between plug colors. NVIS was developed for the military so that soldiers could utilize light in the field without being detected through enemy night vision scopes. I have experience using state-of-the-art Gen III night vision and can tell you that the dimmest of light blooms extremely bright when looking through a scope; *due to the natural infra red spectrum in light.* What NVIS compatible light does is filter out the infra red portion so you can light up a map (etc.) with your goggles on. Another example of its use would be a helicopter pilot flying at night with night vision goggles on. If the control panel inside of the chopper wasn't illuminated with NVIS lighting, the pilot's goggles would go into a protective "auto-darkening mode" to protect from the extreme infra red light bloom. Anyway, I didn't just decide that it was "cool technology", but rather I researched it, tested it and determined that because it only transmits "visible light" it works best for my night fishing application.

Other than lures, the next few items are always carried inside of my plug bag. First item I carry is a leader wallet, which fits nicely between the outer wall of the inserts and inner wall of the bag. Some surfcasters prefer connecting a lanyard to the leader wallet, I do not. Stored in one of my bags side pouches is a spare reel spool as a "just in caser". The rear stack of inserts in my bag is constructed of 9 ½" tall x 3 inch diameter tubes, one of which is always dedicated to a small water bottle and strobe light. My thought process here is that in the event I get caught in a rip, I'm probably going to shed my wading belt first and will reach into my plug bag to grab the water bottle and strobe light for survival and signal purposes before letting it go as well. Call it what you want, I'd rather prepare for the worst than not be prepared at all. What we do is dangerous, no matter where or how we're fishing and the bottom line is that you should always have a plan in the sudden event things turn bad.

Something that seems as if it's never been removed from my "work in progress" category is the gear configuration on my wading belt. Call it SOCD (Surfcasters Obsessive Compulsive Disorder) if you'd like, but I don't think I've ever made it through an entire season without adding, removing or tweaking things an inch or two here and there. This may be a result of coming up in the early days when the "right gear" for our niche surfcasting audience wasn't readily available off the shelf. Because I've always had the ability to fabricate what was needed by hand, half the fun for me has been identifying a need and addressing it the best I possibly could. Although you may not share the same interest or ability to fabricate gear from scratch, I think that part of your formula for success will be to develop an ability to modify gear from its present form so that it best suits your particular needs.

Gear situated on my belt from left to right begins with a titanium tanto (blunt) tip serrated edge dive knife that's held securely by a fixed position horizontally mounted plastic sheath. The knife is protected from accidental loss by a lanyard that's affixed from the sheath to the handle. Most divers, as well as I, prefer using a blunt tip knife to protect against injury should you miss the sheath opening when blindly securing the knife. I prefer titanium because of its strength, light weight and corrosion proof characteristics. If I need to cut myself free in an emergency, which can occur without a moments notice, the knife can be easily accessed with my right hand by reaching across the front of my body, squeezing a clip and sliding it out of its sheath. I have to say that this is one piece of gear that I wouldn't even think of wetsuiting without. Not only are there loose gill nets, monofilament, (etc.) on

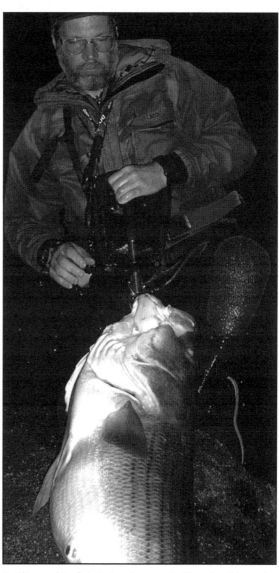

Battling a big fish is hard enough. You should not be fumbling with your gear at the same time.

the ocean floor that you can become entangled with, but your own gear can accidentally become dislodged and caught on the bottom. Should this happen in a swift moving current, an anchoring effect can occur whereas you can be pulled under as whatever's holding you becomes taut. As a side note to this "anchoring effect", never keep a live fish on a long stringer while out on a rock. I know someone who did and almost drowned after the fish swam around the base of the rock a few times and became entangled. After being blown off the rock by a wave he immediately was pulled down by the swift moving current and thankfully was able to cut the rope loose from his belt, *which didn't have a quick release buckle.*

Next in line on my belt is a stainless steel carabiner clip that's welded perpendicular to a plate and bolted in a fixed (non-moveable) position. It's solely dedicated to holding a quality mesh bag with a draw string closure that's sized to comfortably hold a dozen or so eels. Directly next to the carabiner is a stainless steel "D" ring that I use to tether a scotch brite pad with a lanyard. When putting an eel on the hook is required I can utilize the pad to firmly grip the eel, take care of business then drop the pad at my side without fear of losing it. Please note that there are a few other methods I use for gripping a slimy eel when out in the water, but this method is what I most commonly use when on a rock.

To the far left side of my belt (almost behind me) are two "D" rings that are welded to plates in a horizontal and outward facing position. The plates are strategically bolted into position on my belt so that I can seamlessly connect the brass clips that are sewn into the base of my plug bag by reaching upwards and snapping them on. The reason I connect the bag to my belt in this fashion is for an even weight distribution between shoulder and belt. When a plug change is required, I simply unfasten the bag clips from their anchor points and swing the bag in front of myself. A few other advantages of having the bag fastened in this manner are to prevent the bag from swinging around the front of myself when leaning forward to lift a fish from the water and to quickly disconnect the bag when needed during deep water wading or swimming.

Moving on to the right/rear side of my belt is a quality pair of pliers. Contrary to most other surfcaster's preference of 7" titanium, I carry 5 ½" high-grade stainless steel pliers with rubberized grips. I find them to be comparable in weight to the 7" titanium, easier to handle and not as prone to slip out of my wet hands. Just as important, at least for me, is the fact that my pliers are secured in a firm sheath with a lanyard anchoring point to guard against loss. Whatever pliers you choose to utilize, be sure that they're equipped with replaceable side cutter blades.

Something you'll occasionally see on some surfcasters belts, including mine, is a very high quality screw top diver's bottle. The bottle is sealed with an "O" ring and watertight down to depths that far exceed surfcasting requirements. In this bottle I store spare flashlight batteries and hooks. My reasoning for carrying the batteries should be obvious, however, the hooks may not be. Because my bags are built with some added room between the inserts, I've learned the trick of carrying a few extra plugs without hooks in case they're needed. For instance, let's say you fill your inserts with the usual array of lures, but dread losing that trusty old yellow darter and black needle because they've been working well. Storing a few backups of each outside or between the inserts can easily be done if they're "hookless". In the event they're needed, simply grab a few hooks out of the bottle and put the spare plugs into service. This is a good tip... don't forget this one!

Last on my belt is a stringer, which I have broken into two parts. Not

Jimmy in his shop.

being a fish eater, it's rarely used, however, you know those "fish orders" we'll all occasionally fill for close friends and family. Anyway, in order to make this job as seamless as possible, I have two carabiner clips bolted towards the front right side of my wading belt that are each dedicated to carrying both parts of my stringer. In order to make this tricky job, which always seems to have to be done in rough water while out on a rock, a bit faster and easier, here's what I do. Before the fish is at my feet I disconnect a ring on the first carabiner clip that has a narrow, flat and 6" long stainless steel stick attached to it. The stick hangs down to around my knee and remains connected to the carabiner clip by a stainless steel snap ring on the other end of a short rope. Between the passing rollers (waves) I quickly lift the fish out of the water, stick the butt end of my rod between my thighs, remove the hook from the fish's mouth then proceed to run the stick in the mouth and out of the gill plate opening. At this point the fish can be laid in the water while I remove the snap hook from my belt carabiner and connect it to the ring that's holding the stick. With the fish well secured on the short (looped) stringer and provided a large wave isn't rolling in, I now connect the short 3-foot stringer to the ring on the 7-foot long one, which is neatly rolled and stored in a separate case (hanging from the second carabiner clip) with the end ring protruding from it. After connecting the two stringers I open the Velcro closure on the long stringers case and send the fish off swimming. As I mentioned earlier, a live fish shouldn't be left on a stringer while you continue fishing for reasons other than the "shark factor". Instead, I'll now secure my gear and swim the fish in while either keeping the stringer clipped to my belt or in hand. Sound confusing? I apologize if my method's poorly illustrated, but the point that I would much rather get across to you is that having a plan for everything you'll be faced with is extremely important. In this particular case, fumbling with a stringer should be out of the question, as a poor plan can result in either the loss of the fish during a pinnacle moment or you being swept off the rock while dillydallying with a stringer that's tied in knots.

ADDITIONAL TIP'S

Although not a professional writer, I tried my very best to cover all the bases regarding the importance of personal gear during your quest for that first wall hanger of a bass, as well as consistency in success. Before

A quality rod and reel might be a luxury for a weekend angler but for a wetsuiter, they are necessities.

concluding I'd like to comment on a few other items that may be helpful to you as well. First, I almost always wear gloves when wetsuiting. The gloves I wear are light "framers gloves" with the thumb, index and middle fingers exposed, which makes tying knots easy, yet protects the fingers most susceptible to line cuts because they're covered in full. Cutting gloves is usually not an option because they'll fray over a short period of time, whereas framers gloves are stitched across the top of the finger cutouts. Next, I sometimes will carry a pork rind or water bottle holder on my belt. What will determine whether I do or not is dictated by the method of fishing I primarily intend to do and whether I plan on doing Montauk's "south side death march" or not. If the water bottle is not carried on my belt then, as mentioned earlier, it's stored in one of my plug bag inserts. As far as the pork rind, that too is stored in a sealed bag inside of my plug bag if not on my belt. As long as the rind isn't exposed to the air it will remain as supple as it will in the formaldehyde bottle. Last, with the exception of my eel hooks, every barb on all plug hooks gets crushed. My thinking here is that too much can go wrong when you're out on a rock and the last thing I need is a fish to kick the wrong way, lodging a hook in my hand that I can't immediately remove. As a precaution though, I always have a set of "nippers" in the truck that are rated to snap a framing nail in half quickly and easily.

REMAIN FOCUSED WHEN COMPLETING YOUR GEAR PACKAGE

In case you've been wondering "What about rods and reels", I'll have you know that I'm very much set in my ways...with reason though. As a wetsuiter, my needs are defined as requiring shorter than average length graphite surf rods (light to medium action) and reels that are designed and built to do what we do in an extreme way. With requirements not extending beyond these parameters, I have been highly dependant and satisfied with the quality, craftsmanship and level of service delivered by two major manufacturers; Lamiglas and Van Staal. Throughout the years I've solely relied on the performance of custom built one-piece Lami 9'M and 10'L blanks, both having cork tape grips and Fuji guides with plain black on black wraps; *as cosmetics is not my "thing" nor does it help me catch fish*. Each of my rods wouldn't be complete without current VS200 or 250 spinning reels. My recommendation to you is "become one" with whatever spinning or conventional outfit you choose and don't go overkill on the size. In other words, there's a certain "feel" that can only be acquired over time, one that may someday mean the difference between hooking and landing that cow or going home empty handed. As far as line goes, most surfcasters have turned to using braid because of its long cast and sensitive attributes. I've personally tried all current brands of braid and have chosen to stick with monofilament when wetsuiting.

I hope the information I've shared will someday be as helpful to you as it was when shared with me during my early days in Montauk. As I've learned throughout the years, extending your thought process beyond location, lure type and tide sometimes make all the difference in the world. Realizing that there's a certain history in this sport lying deep within our gear, I'd like to express my sincere thanks to Zeno for allowing me this opportunity to share the how and why we use what we do for the sport we love.

CHAPTER SIX

ANGLER'S ETHICS IN THE MODERN WORLD

By William "Doc" Muller

There are some ethical considerations for anglers to consider within the unique, complex, and sometimes threatening circumstances of the "new millennium". Certainly the world of beach fishermen was simpler and the beaches less crowded fifty or sixty years ago while today's complex world is more difficult to negotiate. Today, anglers consider four-wheel drive courtesy, angling etiquette, expensive and dwindling gasoline supplies, and a greater awareness of the role we play to stabilize the ecology of our planet. We could discuss many of these in depth from leaking gas tanks to piping plovers, but for this chapter we'll zero-in on one consideration: catch and release.

Certainly, harvesting fish and wildlife for personal consumption is a valid and significant part of the outdoor experience. Yet, we must also recognize that times have changed and so have our responsibilities. Forty years ago few, if any, anglers thought about stewardship. Rather, many if not most anglers kept everything they caught but at the same time fish resources were more abundant. There were also only about three and a half billion people on the planet in the mid 20th century compared to something around eight billion today; give or take a few hundred million. Then too, the suburbs have exploded. My point is that things change and it would be disrespectful to our sport and the fish we profess to love if we were to turn away from these issues pretending nothing had changed. The old saying is that ostriches do that, but people should not.

Another consideration comes from data released by The Atlantic States Marine Fisheries Commission. According to the ASMFC, the east coast population of striped bass has declined from 66 million pounds to about 55 million pounds. Another data point shows that the spawning female biomass has declined about 26% since a peak in 2003. Tens of millions of fish in the migration may seem to be adequate, but a loss of eleven million pounds of fish is significant. Remember, these fish are spread out in the ocean from the Carolinas to Nova Scotia. That's a lot of water! So, on average, each location will have fewer fish, the schools will be fewer and smaller, and that equates to more difficult angling conditions.

MODERN PRESSURE AND THE OLD ANGLING RITUAL

Consider my angling ritual from decades ago. I fished actively for many species each year including stripers, blues, weakfish, flounder, fluke, porgies, seabass, kingfish, cod, ling, blackfish, and pollock. Today, I fish for fewer species because many species, such as flounder, aren't worth fishing for anymore. In my old ritual, I focused on each species at different times in the season. I never fished for stripers until mid May because I was too busy catching flounders or weakfish, and in good weakfish years my pursuit of stripers receded into June.

In fact, it would be fair to say that I didn't focus on stripers and blues until the fall run and that usually started with an abundant and long mullet run. Today, the stocks of abundant species, such as stripers and blues, are pressured from one end of the season to the other, and the pressure on marine ecosystems stressful. Human pressure may only be appreciated with a perspective of the past when there were far fewer anglers and a lot more fish. Therefore, anglers today can't afford to be passive harvesters like our predecessors; we need to be thoughtful and informed harvesters.

I guess my dad was ahead of his time, because even in the 1940s he'd say to me, "put that one back and we'll catch it next year when it's bigger." I was a child who wanted to bring home fish to show to my mother and grandmother who, in my fantasy, would praise me for my great angling prowess. Yes, my dad was ahead of his time and he started me thinking about conservation and my role in the universe at a very tender age. He's long gone, but I thank him for that head start almost everyday.

THE THOUGHTFUL PROCESS

According to long-time friend and angler Roger Martin, the process of being a responsible steward of our resources should begin long before a fish is caught. He cautions anyone who'll listen that trying to make a decision at the moment of the catch is difficult and awkward because of the adrenaline rush, the chaos of the moment, and the lack of time. He's right, of course.

In my latest book, *"Fishing With Bucktails"*, I make the following suggestion to anglers in the spirit of conservation: "don't kill them for ego, don't kill them because they're legal, and don't kill them for someone else." I didn't put those words in the book to demean anyone who keeps a fish now and then, but rather to heighten awareness of our roles as sportsmen, stewards, and conservationists.

Indeed, if we prepare in advance we are much more likely to make a good decision instead of getting caught up in the moment. The best way to prepare for that moment is to ask some questions. These might include, do I want to clean fish after a long trip? Do I want to eat this fish? Would I like there to be an abundance of stripers for my children and grandchildren

Large fish often exhaust themselves during the fight. Give them proper support and extra time to recover.

to catch and enjoy? Have I already kept enough stripers this year? Was over-harvest one of the reasons for the precipitous decline of stripers in the 1970s? Could it happen again? Which is a better experience: a bad-looking dead fish in my cooler, or the vibrant memory of releasing a big fish that could spawn again and please another angler? These are some of the questions that a good steward of the seas asks and then answers so that at the moment of decision there is clarity. The following discussion is intended to provide anglers with accurate information about how to release fish, the use of appropriate tackle, and other factors that contribute to a good decision and proper release.

MYTHS ABOUT RELEASE

Let's begin by dismissing a number of popular myths about catch and release that sometimes become excuses for not releasing fish. As I offer this information I have my marine biologist hat on in order to lend some credibility to my words. These are myths that I hear on the beach all the time and, in the 21st century there's no way these myths should still have life. Unfortunately, since our public schools offer virtually no outdoor education, it's difficult to expose the myths. Oh yes, our youngsters are taught some environmental science, but environmental science isn't outdoor education. Environmental science concerns environmental problems, their causes, and engineering-based solutions. Outdoor education on the other hand, teaches young people about ecosystems, wildlife, fisheries, and time-honored practices where humans interact with wild life via hunting and fishing.

When I taught ecology at the college level, my students were shocked to learn that if it hadn't been for hunters and fishermen we probably wouldn't have a conservation ethic, support as many national, state, and local parks, or have protected so many creatures from extinction. Incidentally, the father of our conservation ethic was President Theodore Roosevelt and, guess what, his interest evolved out of his love of hunting and fishing. When he realized how many species were diminishing in numbers at the turn of the 20th century and how fast we were expanding our cities, roads, and industry he set about protecting endangered species such as the American Bison and establishing many parks and wildlife refuges. If we don't teach our young people about the outdoors they grow up believing hunters and fishermen are simply cruel people who hurt and kill things for pleasure. Furthermore, unless someone takes them fishing they don't know the difference between a striped bass and a giraffe in spite of the fact that striped bass are engrained in American culture since colonial times. Proper outdoor education can teach students that interaction with fish and wildlife is an appropriate part of our history, culture, and our leisure time pursuits. So, let's dispel some myths, shall we.

"ALL CAUGHT FISH DIE"

I can't even begin to conceive how someone, in this day and age, can believe this. If there's been one there's been a hundred reports, television shows, and documentaries that provide data from returns of tagged fish, the success of catch and release in many fisheries, and data from The American Littoral Society and The Atlantic States Marine Fisheries Commission that show mortality rates for released stripers are typically quite low. The highest mortality results when inexperienced anglers release fish. Thus, we can reduce

It's easier to release fish in calmer waters, but with proper adjustments, jetty jockeys and rough water anglers can do it too.

mortality by educating anglers about the proper way to release fish. Studies show that among experienced anglers with the proper tackle, that mortality of released fish is less than 15% and often a single digit percentage: one thing for sure, a fish in a cooler has 100% mortality. Can we finally put this myth into the grave?

"IF A FISH BLEEDS, IT DIES"

This is another ludicrous myth. Each of us has been cut at one time or another. If the cut was on a finger, your lip, or your scalp you probably bled quite a bit. Did you die? Of course not, so why should a fish. Blood from a fish's lip, mouth, or side of the mouth is a superficial loss of blood and unless a fish develops an infection (a rare occurrence) it is of no consequence. Blood goes a long way. That is, when you mix even a small amount of blood with water it looks like a much larger volume of blood. A problem does arise when a fish bleeds profusely and for a long time. Under such conditions they could lose too much blood, go into shock, and die. Profuse bleeding usually involves wounds to the gills and deep hooks in the throat or gut. Although some fish die when the line is cut and the hook remains deeply set, more fish survive than die and that beats the 100% mortality of kept fish. Attempting to retrieve a hook that costs a few pennies from the throat or gut of a fish makes no sense and usually causes the fish to die. So cut the line, leave the hook in place, and give the fish a chance.

Hooks in gills are handled differently. Trebles in the gills are very difficult to remove without causing major damage because as you loosen one of the hook points one of the other hook points inevitably gets stuck. This is one of many, many reasons why I use bucktails so much. A single hook in a gill can usually be removed without causing major damage. I always carry nine-inch needle nose pliers on my belt for this purpose. Here's how to remove that hook. Don't go in through the mouth, rather lift the gill cover with a finger and look for the hook lodged either over or in a gill arch. Carefully grab the bend of the hook with your needle nose pliers and back it out of or away from the gill arch. Now rotate the bend ninety degrees and push the hook forward into the mouth cavity. Pull gently on your leader or turn the fish upside down and the bucktail falls out. Typically, there is little or no bleeding when this method is used with care.

"THERE'S TOO MANY BASS"

I've even heard this one from some fisheries managers who seem to think it's a better idea to reduce the number of predators rather than manage baitfish species more appropriately. Managers tell us they are attempting to create a better balance between predators and prey. I have a better idea: stop allowing the harvest of small fishes, shrimp, squid, and the rest. Bunker comes to mind when I think of this conundrum involving prey and predators.

Consider a time-honored criterion for fisheries management that sets size limits to allow fish to reach sexual maturity before they are harvested. Nowadays, we should also consider their value as food for other fishes. Furthermore, science has proven that it is more efficient to allow fish to grow to larger sizes before harvest because the total yield in pounds is greater than when we harvest the little ones. Yet, when it comes to bunker, commercial bunker boats are allowed to keep bunker of all sizes. In Chesapeake Bay, for example, this practice has reduced the biomass of small bunker so much that some experts have suggested there aren't enough small food items in the bay to sustain smaller stripers. I challenge managers to institute regulations that make sense and protect small fishes and the young of various bait species from premature harvest. More food for stripers means more of them can be sustained. Let's get our ducks in a row, shall we? Although we can convince ourselves of all sorts of complicated things, in the end common sense usually works best.

"ONCE A FISH IS CAUGHT IT WILL NEVER EAT AGAIN"

Wow! I won't dignify this one by trying to argue against it. Instead I'll offer a story or two and you decide which side of the argument makes sense. It was a fall run of big blues in the 1980s. John Fritz and I didn't catch much on the morning tide, but in the afternoon we found the blues waiting along the National Seashore. We were chunking that day and John was very fussy about his bait rigs. He made them himself and they were unique. Well, John had a pick up, set the hook, but he lost the fish because another fish cut the line. A few minutes later I had a fish on and when I landed it there was John's shiny hook stuck in its mouth with the rest of his special rig trailing away from the jaw.

Appropriate tackle allows us to manage the fight better and reduces the length of the battle and that means a greater chance for a successful release.

Need another example? I was fishing in Long Island Sound 20 years ago and catching schoolies when a pod of small blues intruded. I caught one blue that I took notice of because it had a cut on its side right above the anal fin and it had a black spot; about the size of a dime, along the lateral line mid way to the tail on its left side. I released it, but caught it again minutes later. I released it again but caught it again several minutes later. By now, the hook had created several holes and there was some minor bleeding and its lower lip had peeled away from the bone a bit. I released it and caught it again about five minutes later complete with dangling lower lip. As the saying goes, "don't believe everything you read in the papers" and in this case don't believe the silly myths about catch and release. In truth, the key to successful release is found in the tackle we use and a correct method of releasing fish.

TACKLE

Many anglers seem to be indifferent about the tackle they use. For me, on the other hand, my tackle components are my tools and, as any good carpenter will tell you, you need good tools to do a good job. I don't know, maybe I'm just weird. Check that, I know what you're thinking and yes, I'm am a little weird, but that's irrelevant to my point. Technology has made great tackle affordable to most folks and great tackle is great tackle because it's durable, precise, tough, and kind of blends with your hands. Truly, the right tackle makes the skills of angling easier to achieve. The same technology has also revolutionized light tackle. Equipment that was once just wimpy and frail now boasts many of the same abilities as sturdier tackle from past decades.

In the last ten years or so there's been a "light tackle" craze sweeping the coastlines of this country. It has opened up new angling opportunities and exciting presentations. However, saltwater light tackle fishing doesn't mean taking a fresh water rod and reel and using it to catch larger and more powerful saltwater fish. Fortunately, tackle companies have adapted light tackle angling to saltwater and today's light tackle may be light in weight but it isn't flimsy. It has power, provides casting and fish fighting control, and does not; in and of itself, create extended battles. With today's technology fish can be dispatched quickly and efficiently in order to minimize stress and maximize angling fun and success. However, it should be noted that anglers own a responsibility to care for the striper resource and the following discussion about tackle is intended to provide us with some insight.

Shock from excessive blood loss or a prolonged fight is the most common reason why released fish don't survive. When fish fight too long they begin to build up wastes in their muscles including lactic acid. Normally, glucose is oxidized for energy in muscles and the process derives energy and gives off carbon dioxide and water. However, when muscles run low on oxygen, such as during a prolonged fight, the muscles take a sort of shortcut by engaging in animal fermentation rather than oxidation. The result is less energy derived and lactic acid builds up in the muscles. If enough wastes build up, physiological mechanisms attempt to adjust and to some extent are successful, but if the process goes too far the fish begins to enter a condition known as shock. If the shock is too severe or prolonged, then the fish will enter a state called irreversible shock and will die. A fish in mild shock that isn't released properly may die as many as three days later, while one that is in irreversible shock will die quickly. Using the right tackle and the right angling approach will prevent a fish from going into permanent shock, and I believe is an angler's responsibility.

In most surf fishing situations we need to make long casts and toss heavy lures and sinkers. That means we are most often restricted from using light tackle. To this day, when my back allows me, I prefer to use my eleven-foot Lamiglass 1M rod and either a Van Staal 300 or 250 spooled with thirty-pound test braided line. This outfit provides a "best blend" of tackle characteristics. It has power, I can manage fish of all sizes, I can make long casts with lures of a wide span of weights, I am able to deal with adverse conditions of waves and winds, and I can battle the fish to the beach long before it goes into shock. These are the reasons why I use this outfit whenever I'm able to, even in quiet waters. However, in quiet waters with little influence from waves and winds, an angler may elect a smaller outfit. For reasons of angling comfort and stewardship, I would not recommend the use of anything smaller in the surf than a nine-foot graphite rod. I prefer the Lamiglass 1M nine-foot rod with a Van Staal 200 and spooled with twenty-pound test braided line. The Van Staal reels are not only dependable but also are powerhouses that allow an angler to pressure a fish with the gears of the reel as well as the power of the blank.

Fishing shouldn't just be about "us", it should also be about the fish, the habitats, the sunrise, the waves, the shorebirds, and everything else that comes with the package. If we can step outside ourselves perhaps we can better understand the responsibilities that evolve from this richness of our outdoor experience.

THE DIGITAL CAMERA

There's one more piece of equipment that could, in the modern world, be considered an element of tackle since we can use it to record our catches without the need to kill a fish. Of course, I'm talking about modern cameras that are small, compact, light weight, and take top quality photos. These cameras, whether conventional film or digital versions, can easily be tucked into a wader pouch, a sweatshirt pocket, or even into a side pouch of you're your tackle bag because many cameras are compact and waterproof.

Perhaps digital cameras offer the best option since we can see the photo immediately after taking it. If we don't like the photo we can take another and another until it's right. Furthermore, when we get home we can download the information into our computer, print out copies, and setup our own photo file. The availability of a digital camera might cause some anglers to think twice about keeping a big striper since a rich memory of the fish will be safely tucked away in the camera.

HOW TO RELEASE FISH PROPERLY

If an angler has previously thought about fish they might wish to keep and those they might wish to release the decision on the beach will be simple and quick. If an angler has correctly erased the notions generated by mythology, uses appropriate tackle and fights a fish properly, then a valid choice will be available to the angler. So, before moving on, let's assume the thought process has been done, the tackle is good, the fight proper, and the drag set at one-third the strength of the line, and finally that you wish to release this fish.

We also need to consider the differences between places we fish. For instance, it's easier to release fish on a beach with calm seas, and more difficult to release them from jetties and rocks in rough seas unless you are committed to taking the time to adjust to conditions and do it right. Given all these elements, let's look at how to do it.

GET IT BACK INTO THE WATER FAST:

First, get the fish back into the water as fast as possible. This is the most important element of a successful release. A good rule of thumb is to hold your breath as the fish comes out of the water and, when you can't hold your breath anymore, assume the fish can't either. That means, if you need to dunk the fish in the water for a while as you attempt to recover your oxygen level, do so. I've watched anglers fuss for many minutes removing a stubborn hook from jaw cartilage trying not to tear the mouth, only to discover that when the fish is released it goes belly up. Fish are able to repair wounds just as we are, but once they suffocate they're dead. It may

When reviving a tired fish, support it upright both in front and towards the tail for best results.

seem counter-intuitive but tear the hook out of the mouth if necessary, and get that fish back into the water fast!

DON'T STEP ON A FISH:

If you don't know how to handle a fish, or you are afraid of it or hooks, then don't fish until you learn how to handle fish safely and properly. Please, I implore you to never step on a fish while you attempt to unhook it. It's just common sense. How would you like the "Jolly Green Giant" to step on you in his cornfield? You wouldn't, and he'd probably damage your internal organs. So, never step on a fish!

NEVER KICK A FISH INTO THE WATER:

Tell me, does a fish look like a football? If the "Jolly Green Giant" kicked you across the cornfield, would you like it? If you respect your sport and the fish you fish for, then take a moment and lift the fish gently with a hand and toss it gently back into the water.

LITTLE FISH

Little fish may be removed from the hook and tossed into the water. That doesn't mean a moon-shot so that the fish splats on the water. However, a gentle underhand toss from a foot above the water does no harm and some research suggests it may actually stimulate the fish to move and breathe. Practice this and you'll find you'll get good at timing it so the fish's head enters the water first and almost parallel to the surface of the water while facing away from you.

WALK A BIG ONE

Larger fish require more help and so do fish that fight on light tackle. Fish that fight for a long time require more help too, regardless of size (hence the importance of a proper drag setting). Placing the fish in the water and supporting it while it recovers is often referred to as "walking the fish". The proper way to support a fish is to use one hand around the base of the tail and the other under its head while keeping the fish upright in the water. Either move the fish back and forth in the water or walk forward to move water into its mouth and out its gills.

INDICATORS

There are several indicators you can use to judge a fish's readiness for release. These include the erectness of the dorsal fin, the fish's ability

The richness of surf fishing can be found in many facets of the sport: not just filling a cooler. Beautiful twilights, shore birds, the rhythm of the waves, and the brotherhood of anglers are important too. (Photo by Dennis Wolf)

to remain upright, and its muscle tension. A fish that's in trouble is quite pliable and cannot remain upright and the dorsal fin is flat along the top of the body. As a fish recovers and its blood oxygen level returns towards normal, the dorsal fin begins to stand up, the fish remains upright without help, and muscle activity can be detected via a sense of tension transmitted to your hand. Eventually, the fish will try to pull out of your hands. Be warned. A fish will initially try to pull out of your hand a little before it's ready, so hang onto it another minute before releasing it. That little bit of extra time makes a big difference.

PATIENCE

You'll need patience for some fish. Be a good steward of the seas by temporarily forgetting about your next fish and concentrating on doing a good job of releasing the one in your hands. Some fish recover in a minute, some in several minutes, and some take a bit longer. Be patient. A fish that's released before the three vital indicators have corrected will likely mean that the fish, although it swims off, will die within three days.

BEST MEMORIES

You now have all you need to execute a philosophy of conservation and be a good steward of our sea's resources as you participate in the great sport of surf fishing for striped bass: a pre-decision, proper tackle, the right drag, a good fight plan, and a solid release method. As I said earlier, each person's decision about whether or not to keep a fish is a personal one, but the reasons for your decision shouldn't, in my opinion, be made without a careful and thoughtful process. We should be armed with the information to make it work. I want lots of stripers for my grandkids to catch and that's just one reason why I'm so adamant about catch and release. Perhaps my fervor is also a result of having lived through the "great collapse" of the fishery in the 1970s and 80s, and I know how easily it could happen again. Perhaps it's an outgrowth of my observations over the years at how easily people kill things without ever considering the consequences. But, and this is a big but, it's also very much about my catch and release memories. A dead fish is ugly and soon forgotten. I've released several fish well over fifty pounds and each release still shines brightly in my memory even though much time has passed. I take great pleasure in the thought that I don't have to kill and I can revel in the memories of many, many big fish swimming away to breed again and fight again.

Stripers are majestic fish and the species has not only been important to millions of surf anglers, it's also an integral part of the history of the east coast of this country going back to colonial days. For me, this majesty deserves majestic respect.

CHAPTER SEVEN

LIVE EELS

By John Skinner

"Last cast," I announced to myself, as I fired a yellow darter into the darkness from the tip of a South Shore jetty. I was tired enough that I was hoping the plug would make it back to the rocks without being intercepted, as it had been numerous times during the preceding hours by stripers into the 20-pound class. The last 45 minutes had been uneventful, and if I hustled, I could probably squeeze a few hours of sleep out of the night. I shared the tip with Scott, an angler who I had crossed paths with a few times before. He was throwing live eels and had only one fish to show for his efforts, but his fish was slightly larger than my best for the night. He could have those few extra pounds, I thought, as I had no interest in buying, caring for, or fishing with the slimy creatures. I'd much rather throw wood or plastic.

The plug did indeed make it to the jetty unscathed this time. I hung it on the frame of my gathering guide and rock hopped to where my surf bag was positioned, well away from where it could be splashed by waves breaking on the rocks. "You calling it a night?" asked Scott, with an odd hint of hopefulness in his voice. "Yeah, I haven't had a touch in a while, and I could use some sleep. "Have a safe drive home," he responded, with what I now interpreted as enthusiasm.

The crunching of korker spikes told me he was making a move, but I didn't think much of it as I gathered my gear together and began heading off the jetty with a bass I had kept. I stopped dead in my tracks at the sound of ZZZZZT, the unmistakable sound of the slip of a tight drag on a hard hookset. I turned around to see Scott's silhouette leaning back on a heavily bent rod while he stood on the very rock I had just vacated. "That didn't take you long," I offered, in what probably came across as an annoyed tone. "It's a good one," he answered in a strained voice, but I already knew that by the sound of his drag as line melted from his spool. I laid my gear down and walked over to see what I had missed and lend some help if he wanted it. He was well equipped with beefy tackle, and put the fish at the base of the rocks in less than 10 minutes. I had the "pleasure" of dropping down to the water's edge and lip-gaffing the trophy that I couldn't help but think had seen my plug numerous times.

I handed the gaff to Scott, and he pulled the fish to the top of the jetty. When I made it back up the rocks, I saw that he had laid it near my fish. My 22-pounder looked like a schoolie next to his. I was not at all surprised to hear him announce "44 pounds" as he hung it on his scale. Sensing how I felt, he pointed at his fish and then my plug while saying "fish like this usually don't hit those things". Well, that one certainly didn't, but it took only a single cast with a live eel for the fish to strike.

Whatever sleep I could have had before work that morning was ruined by the thoughts of that fish and the words of the other angler. Sure, it was

John Skinner learned long ago that big fish often strike eels when they won't touch a plug.

possible that I had just walked away at the wrong time, and the cow showed up as Scott jumped on that rock, but I didn't believe that. There was current, and the fish was most likely holding in an eddy that set up there. It probably watched my plugs go by dozens of times and didn't react until it saw the eel. I hated the thought of having to go through the expense and inconvenience of dealing with live eels, but the night had convinced me that it would be necessary if I wanted to be successful with truly large bass. Within less than a year, I eeled my first forty-plus.

There was an obvious lesson to be learned from that night - big fish often hit eels when they won't hit plugs, but as years passed, and my experience grew, my entire approach to targeting trophy stripers changed.

TROPHY FISHING PHILOSOPHY

When I first started fishing, I had a preoccupation with baitfish. I focused a lot on where the bunker, mullet, baby weakfish, sandeels, or anything else that might attract stripers would be. I never made a conscious decision to stop worrying about bait, it just happened as I grew more experienced with catching big bass on a consistent basis. One day while listening to a seminar lecture about baitfish movements, I realized that when it came to targeting quality bass on the night tides, I gave absolutely no thought to bait. Sure, if I was fooling around with schooling fish on the open beaches during the fall, I wanted to know where those peanut bunker or herring were. But the rest of my fishing forgot about baitfish long ago.

Accurate or not, somewhere along the way I began to believe that bass over 30 pounds spent a very small percentage of their time actively feeding. The rest of the time they were probably in a neutral feeding mode. I imagine they suck down a porgy, sea robin, blackfish, fluke, or whatever fairly large meal they find, and they don't expend additional energy looking for food on a full belly. In my mind, maybe they're feeding an hour a day. What are they doing for the other 23 hours? They're staging somewhere. With the exception of migration times, are they likely to stage in random different places, or are they habitual, and hanging out in the same areas when not feeding? Of course, because of the tides, they live in a somewhat ever-changing environment, but those changes are cyclic and predictable. A tide calendar and localized experience is all that we need in order to know where and when a potentially attractive feature such as an eddy will set up. While it's unlikely that neutral resident bass will sit in the same spots all of the time, it might be possible to predict where some will be with fairly dependable consistency.

Let's pretend this is all true. Bass will spend a small portion of their time feeding. At that time, they're going to seek out food. They're not picky. Anyone who has gutted a few bass will tell you that there is very little they *won't* eat. Although they'd love a big bunker, they often don't seem all that

Big stripers spend most of their time in a neutral or non-feeding mode, yet they still find a live eel hard to resist.

willing to swim to where the bunker are. That's why the boat guys on Long Island's South Shore often net their live bunker baits well back in the bays near the rivers and creeks, and then speed to the inlet areas to liveline them for bass. If the bass were motivated enough to go where the bunker are, then those boats could just stay and fish the bunker schools. Instead, it seems that the bigger bass are lazy. They eat what's nearby, and then they hang out in areas where they feel comfortable. That comfort might be provided by things like a desired water temperature, oxygenation, salinity, a feeling of safety, or the knowledge that they probably won't have to go far for the next meal.

So in my mind, bass that aren't on a migration will spend the majority of their time in a neutral feeding mode in the same general areas on the same portions of the tide. But there's an obvious problem for those of us trying to catch these fish – they aren't in a feeding mood. This is where the power of a live eel comes in – bass will often hit an eel when they're not actively feeding. I believe the 44-pounder that I mentioned at the beginning of this chapter is an example. That fish was holding in an eddy. It wasn't hungry enough to hit my plugs, but it couldn't pass up an eel. I have no trouble relating to this scenario.

I don't spend a very large portion of my day eating, and of course, most people don't. But I have a weakness. I could be comfortably satiated, but put a free slice of pizza in front of me, and it's gone. I simply don't have the willpower to pass up a slice. I believe bass are the same way with eels, and that feeling was cemented one night on Montauk's South Side.

I was fishing a point that's a fair walk from Camp Hero, and there were two anglers about 75 yards to my east. I was into fish on eels, and doing my best to keep my light off so that I wouldn't advertise my success and invite company. I had just landed a decent fish in the high twenties, and when I ran my hand down the leader into its mouth to pop the hook out, I hit something strange. I turned my light on briefly to see what I was dealing with. To my amazement, a sizeable bluefish tail was sticking out of the throat of the bass. I slowly and carefully pulled the bluefish out and realized that it weighed somewhere between two and three pounds. The bass looked like it was choking on the fish. It couldn't possibly have been hungry, and couldn't swallow anything even if it was, but it still hit my eel.

I've read theories that bass hit eels not only for food, but also out of some grudge they hold against them because of their interaction with eels on the striper spawning grounds. I have no idea if there's anything to support this, but I do know that the bass I caught with the bluefish stuck in its throat hit an eel it couldn't eat.

Whether or not what I believe with respect to bass behavior is accurate, it influences how I fish, and my approach to targeting large bass with eels has worked very well for me. It's a simple objective – put a live eel in front of a big bass, and most of the time, you'll be provided with an opportunity. Then it's up to your gear and experience to convert that opportunity into a landed fish.

Getting the eel in front of a trophy fish is the hard part. Unless you have the luck of a Lotto winner, you're not going to find 40s giving themselves away while they roll on the surface. You need to put a lot of time in under a wide range of conditions and cover a fair amount of productive looking territory until big fish patterns become apparent. These patterns exist. You can bet that any surf angler who puts big fish on the beach consistently has one or more dependable patterns under his belt in which he *knows* he'll be on big fish given the right set of conditions. You can also bet that

Although live eels can be productive during daytime hours, they really shine at nighttime.

his pattern will be a closely guarded secret.

The best time of the year to use eels is anytime bass are around. Most eel casting is done between dusk and dawn, but they will also take fish during the daylight hours. Where's a good place to start? Absolutely anywhere you know 20-pound plus bass have been landed with some regularity within eel casting distance of the shore. An eel is probably the best tool a surf angler can use to locate fish. Bass find them hard to resist, and because they're fished in a manner similar to lures, it's easy to cover a lot of ground while fishing with them.

DON'T MISS YOUR CHANCE

It goes without saying that you can't land a fish that you can't hook. I think the vast majority of encounters with large stripers last only a second or two, because the angler is unable to bury the hook into the rock-hard mouth. The bigger the fish, the more difficult the task becomes. Even if you do your homework and do everything right and are rewarded with the hit of a trophy bass, it's all wasted if you can't penetrate the hook. These are rare opportunities that are the result of a lot of invested time and hard work, and everything possible must be done to ensure that you maintain contact with the fish. This philosophy drives my gear choices. Fishing with a graphite rod and a needle-sharp hook connected to braided line that's spooled on a reel with a very tight drag goes a long way toward closing the deal.

Let's consider what happens when you set the hook on a fish that's a hundred feet away. Keep in mind that a hundred feet is well short of the eel-casting limit under most conditions. When you lean back to set the hook, much of the energy of the hookset is absorbed by the bend of the rod, the belly in the line caused by the wind and/or tide, the stretch of the line, and the slip of your drag if you've managed to make firm enough contact for your reel's drag to give. Whatever hook setting force is left on the fish's end has to be enough to sink the hook into the bony mouth of a large striper. This is a creature that has adapted from slurping small baitfish as a schoolie to grabbing sea robins and crabs. If you carefully inspect the mouth of a bass over 30 pounds, you'll wonder how we're ever successful. But there is much we can do to help tilt the odds in our favor.

Before the introduction of braided superlines in the mid '90s, I was accustomed to losing about a quarter of my eeling hookups within the first few seconds. I'd set the hook, the fish would thrash on top, and then it was off. I accepted this as unavoidable and business as usual. I switched from monofilament to braided line soon after it hit the market. Within the first season I noticed two things – I almost never dropped a fish that I stuck, and my percentage of fish over 35 pounds went up significantly.

Superbraid lines, such as Power Pro and Spiderwire Stealth, offer many advantages over monofilament. Braid has a much higher strength to diameter ratio. Where I used to use 20-pound-test monofilament, I now use 50-pound-test braid, but the braid has the diameter of 12-pound-test mono. So I'm using a much thinner line with well over twice the breaking strength. Braid is far more abrasion-resistant than monofilament, and this has saved many large fish for me in rocky areas. If a fish does take me around a rock, I back way down on the drag pressure and just let the fish run. If you've ever tried to cut braided line, you know that it's difficult to do if it's not under pressure. This also applies when the line is rubbing against a rock. The fish may take a fair amount of line, but it will tire from the run. At that point, I'll start pumping the line back by alternating my left hand between cupping the spool on each lift of the rod, and cranking the line on the drop. Amazingly, the line has almost always come back undamaged from these exercises.

Perhaps the most important quality of braided line with respect to converting strikes to landed fish is its lack of stretch. The stretch of monofilament line dampens its sensitivity and absorbs much of the power of a hookset. Braided lines have almost no stretch. When braid first hit the market, I immediately began using it for bucktailing. I found it so sensitive compared to mono that I was a bit hesitant to use it for live eel fishing. I began thinking if I felt the fish so easily, maybe the fish felt the tension on the line and would drop the eel. The best way to find out was to try it, and once I did, I quickly corrected my thinking and never went back.

Most of my live eel fishing is split between two outfits. The first is an 11-foot graphite rod based on a Lamiglas GSB1321M blank. It's matched with a Penn 706Z spooled with 50-pound braid. The rod has excellent stopping power, and will comfortably throw eels to over 20 inches. The second rod is a 9-footer that is based on a 10-foot Lamiglas GSB1201L blank with one foot cut from the butt. The rod was recommended to me by John Schauer, an expert rod builder. He called this his "Montauk Eel Rod". Coupled with a Van Staal 200 spooled with 30-pound Spiderwire Stealth, the rod has a deceptive ability to muscle large fish from boulder-strewn areas.

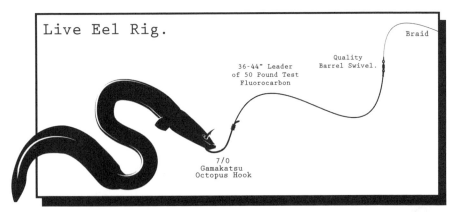

Live Eel Rig.

Braid

Quality Barrel Swivel.

36-44" Leader of 50 Pound Test Fluorocarbon

7/0 Gamakatsu Octopus Hook

Keep your eel rig simple, a 36- to 44-inch leader of 50-pound-test fluorocarbon with a quality barrel swivel and a 7/0 Gamakatsu Octopus hook.

The terminal end of the tackle is simple – a 36- to 44-inch leader of 50-pound-test fluorocarbon with a quality barrel swivel on one end and a 7/0 Gamakatsu Octopus hook on the other. I can't overstate the importance of using a high-quality chemically sharpened hook such as those manufactured by Gamakatsu and Owner. These hooks are very sharp right out of the package, and they have a tendency to stay sharp. I check my hook points frequently, and if I find one that's not perfect, it goes in the trash. In the overall scheme of fishing expenses, I'm not going to risk missing the fish of a season, or lifetime, because I tried to save fifty cents on a hook. I'm careful to never remove these hooks from fish with pliers. Doing so can weaken a hook, leading to breakage. I hook eels through the lower jaw and out just behind an eye socket and use burlap rags for handling the eels. These rags become slimed up and ineffective after a trip or two, so I buy burlap in large rolls found in garden supply stores.

SHALLOW WATER EELING

Whether I'm fishing the Montauk rocks, Long Island's North Shore, or the open ocean beaches, my approach to fishing with live eels is very similar. The eel is cast and then retrieved slowly with the rod held at a higher than normal angle. Hits normally come as a couple of sharp bumps, as if someone slapped the tip of the rod. When I feel this, I drop the rod tip to a lower angle, and then set the hook hard when I feel the line tighten. This is similar to what's known as the *bow to the cow* method used by most eel-drifting boat anglers. That first hookset will probably recover enough line belly or move the fish enough for me to crank down and hit the fish again. I'll hit the fish a third time if I can.

When I first started eel casting, I'd react to a hit by knocking the line out of the line roller and free spooling the hit for at least five seconds before striking. This worked much of the time, but too many fish ended up gut-hooked, and a fair number dropped the eel before I tried to set the hook. When I switched to the faster hookset, I saw an overall increase in my hookup percentage, and an almost total elimination of gut-hooked fish. I lost less fish too, probably because the hook was less likely to tear out of the firm jaw area. I also saw a reduction in the number of small fish caught eeling because they weren't able to control the big eels before I snatched them away.

A faster hook set often results in a solid hook up, as the fish does not have a chance to spit out the eel. It also greatly reduces the chance of gut hooking the fish.

I deviate from the more common advice that you should never adjust your drag with a fish on. I fish with my drag nearly locked. When I set the hook, I don't want to hear slippage. The bass I'm eeling for are too big to get out of the box in a hurry. When you hit them, you have a little time before they're able to gain traction and go on a run. After I'm satisfied with the hookset, I'll back down a touch on the drag if I think I need to. I'll almost always back down a little more when the fish is close. This may be a somewhat unorthodox way to deal with drag pressure, but it's what has worked best for me. My attitude is that I'm in much more danger of losing or missing a fish because my drag slipped on the hookset, than I am of the fish breaking my line because of an over-tightened drag.

In relatively shallow and rocky areas, such as the South Side of Montauk, live eels have a nasty habit of swimming down into the bottom structure and vegetation. The livelier the eel, the worse the problem. If I'm in a convenient position to do so, I'll grasp a lively eel by the head, and slap the tail end against the rock I'm standing on. From my experience, this does not in any way diminish the effectiveness of the eel; it simply allows me to work over a cluttered bottom without hanging. I prefer eels in the 15- to 18-inch range for most areas. The larger eels are saved for inlet fishing.

When I catch a fish on an eel, I'll keep using it. It's not uncommon to catch three or more fish on the same eel. Many of my largest fish fell to eels that were beat up by other fish. If I've had an eel on for a long time and think it might be time for a fresh one, I'll grab the head and watch to see if the tail curls. If it does, then I'll keep casting it. I might keep casting it anyway even if it appears dead. Any dead eels from a night of fishing are put in the freezer when I return home so they can be tied into rigged eels.

INLET EELING

Maybe the best shortcut one can use to finding quality stripers is to fish ocean inlets. These channels of water that cut the barrier islands can be counted on to hold fish throughout the season. The life-filled jetties, deep moving water, irregular bottom structure, and the nearly constant passage of food between the bays and the ocean make the inlets a hard place for bass to resist. The challenge is to get an eel into the strike zone and keep it there long enough for a bass to find it. When the water is moving, which is almost all of the time in most inlets, we can be assured that the strike zone is very close to the bottom. Fish can't afford to expend energy fighting fast moving water, so they'll use the bottom structure to break the current. The challenge is to get the eel into the near-bottom strike zone with a natural presentation.

I focus all of my inlet eeling on the periods near or during slack current. In Long Island's eastern South Shore inlets, this window may last anywhere from 15 minutes to two hours depending on the particular jetty and the phase of the moon. The only way to know what to expect is to put your time in on the same inlet until you learn it. Outside of that slow water window, it's possible to find eeling water by concentrating on places where bends in the jetty break the current.

I rely on large eels in the 18- to 22-inch range to get to the near-bottom inlet strike zone. These are strong powerful creatures that can handle the moving water and swim to the bottom. I cast these upcurrent, give them a little slack to swim to the bottom, then I either maintain contact while the

Fishing large eels near slack current is a recipe for success when eeling an inlet.

eel is carried by the current, or I use a very slow retrieve. Once the eel has been carried downcurrent, the force of the water will push it higher into the water column and out of the strike zone. At that point I'll reel it back quickly and make another cast. Because I'm depending on the eel to swim to the bottom, I don't do well with eels that are nearly dead from an extended casting period or from having caught fish.

I fish only unweighted eels. Some anglers deal with the current by using small drail sinkers. These typically work best with smaller eels because casting a large eel and a drail can be difficult. If you cannot get large enough eels for inlet fishing, then the drail and small eel combination is a good alternative.

No matter where you're fishing, if you miss a fish cleanly on a hookset, you've got a good chance of having another crack at the same fish with a well-placed cast to where you had the hit. I'd always felt this was the case, because on numerous occasions, I'd have hits on consecutive casts after having gone a long time without any. I could never prove that the hits came from the same fish until something rather bizarre happened.

I had gone about 90 minutes without a hit, when I lost a fish and my eel after a very brief hookup. I quickly attached another eel and threw it to where I had the hit. Within seconds I was in again. As I got the 20-pound class fish close, I was glad to see that my eel had slid up the line. I was very confused when I reached down to grab the fish and another eel hung from its mouth. Apparently this was the fish I lost on the previous cast, and the tail end of the eel that I lost on that cast was still in the fish's mouth. When I set the hook the second time, I drove the hook through the tail of the first eel and into the fish. So I caught the fish, got both my eels back, and gained some reassurance that I had been right all along about missed fish coming back on subsequent casts.

Unfortunately, bluefish will also exhibit the same behavior. I once had a night of very good bass fishing interrupted by frequent bluefish strikes that were cutting through my eel supply. The interference came to an abrupt end when I landed a single bluefish that had one of my hooks in it that had been cut off an hour earlier. After removing that one fish, I was bluefish-free the rest of the night. Since then, I have switched to plugs on a few occasions to get unwanted bluefish out of the way. I have also dealt successfully with bluefish by taking a short break. Once the scent and sound of food slapping the water was removed, the bluefish moved on. If there are a lot of bluefish in an area, you may have no choice but to fish elsewhere.

Keeping eels in a tank at home allows you to pick the right size eels for a particular set of conditions.

A HOME LIVE WELL

It would be pretty unreasonable to walk into a bait and tackle store and ask for some eels of a certain size, such as the 18- to 22-inchers that I prefer for inlets. This is where having a well stocked home live well becomes important. I usually have several dozen eels in my well, and this allows me to choose the size eels I need for a particular set of conditions I plan to fish.

Eels are amazing creatures. They'll live in salt water, fresh water, or even no water at all as long as you keep them cool and damp. They're really the only convenient large live bait available to surfcasters. If you're serious about fishing live eels, then it's worth setting up a live well at home to keep a high quality and convenient supply available throughout the fishing season.

There are many good reasons for setting up a home live well. For starters, it will save a lot of money in the long run because eels left over from a trip can be kept alive for use at a later date. Taking advantage of that can actually result in more fish being caught over the course of a season. Since you don't have to worry about wasting unused eels at the end of a trip, you're free to bring along a big enough supply to cover situations such as an excellent bite or the presence of bluefish. This can keep you into fish on a night when you might have run out of eels early because you were being cost-conscious about how many to buy for a single trip. Having a supply readily available is also a great convenience since you don't have to stop and buy them before every trip. This is especially beneficial when heading out on hours when the shops are closed.

My eel well is a 30-gallon container with a drain-valve at the bottom for easy water changing. A small plastic garbage can would do just fine. I use fresh water from the garden hose to fill it, and add a couple tablespoons of Better Bait each time I change the water. This product, and ones like it, helps maintain the bait's slime coat. I aerate the water with a fish tank pump. If I have more than 50 eels in the tank and the weather is hot, I'll power up a second pump, although I'm not sure it's necessary. The fish tank pumps are connected to tubing with 6-inch air stones at the ends. I've used larger air stones, but they don't seem to work any better, they're more expensive, and they break easier.

Any pet store that carries tropical fish will likely stock the pumps, tubing, and air stones. If you use an inexpensive trashcan for your main container, you should be able to put together a one-pump setup for about $50. Check with your local bait and tackle shops for the availability of Better Bait. A 3-pound container will last more than a season.

It's best to store eels in a cool place, but it's not at all necessary. I used to think I needed to keep the water from getting very warm on hot days, so I'd drop in a frozen two-liter bottle of water twice a day. This was actually counter-productive. Looking back, I think the fluctuating temperature killed more eels than the heat would have. I don't worry about the hot days anymore. My eels are kept in a detached garage that gets baked in the afternoon sun during the summer. As long as I keep the water sufficiently aerated and keep up with the water changes, the eels cope with the heat just fine.

The frequency of water exchanges varies with the temperature. I may change the water as often as every other day if the weather is very warm. At cooler times of the season I might change it only once a week. Generally, I'll keep an eye on the turbidity of the water and change it when it starts getting very cloudy. Twice weekly water exchanges are usually sufficient under normal conditions.

I never let my eels swim freely in the 30-gallon container. Instead, I confine them to a covered 5-gallon black pail with holes drilled in it. Though cramming a large number of eels into a relatively small bucket sounds like a good way to shorten their survival time, I haven't found this to be true. I noticed that when I used to let them swim freely, they would do just that, and lose weight in the process. Keeping them packed into the smaller bucket restricts their movement and keeps them from getting skinny. They're not very aerodynamic to begin with, and keeping them a bit chunkier makes them easier to cast. Having them already in a bucket is also much more convenient and less damaging than chasing them around with a scoop net before trips.

I prefer to fish with dark eels. I'm not certain how much of a difference this really makes, but it's long been recognized that darker objects produce a more discernable silhouette at night, and that might explain the perceived advantage. Since eels will to some extent take on the color of their surroundings, keeping them in a black bucket makes them a bit darker.

Eels will live for quite some time out of the water as long as you keep them damp and somewhat cool. I transport my eels from home to my fishing destinations in a bucket with holes drilled in the bottom. These drain holes are important so that the eels don't suffocate in their own slime. This bucket is placed in a second bucket to catch the drainage. I normally don't use any ice, but eels will live for a day or two in this setup if sprinkled with some crushed ice. When wade fishing, I keep my eels in a small mesh diving bag tucked under my surf belt. The bag needs to be dunked once in a while to keep the eels from drying out, especially on windy nights. On the jetties, I use a small bucket with holes drilled in the bottom. You'll need a cover for the bucket to keep the raccoons out.

FRAME OF MIND

The most important thing to take with you when you go eel casting is a big fish mindset. You must make a commitment to stick with the technique and accept the fact that you might have to endure hours of hitless fishing to have a shot at a quality fish. This requires ignoring the smaller fish that are often readily available with other methods. This can be difficult in the beginning, but with patience and determination, you'll eventually catch quality bass. By putting time in under varied conditions, patterns will begin to emerge. By planning your trips around these patterns, you'll be fishing with your most important weapon – confidence. Once you have confidence, and you're convinced that it's only a matter of time before you tie into another big fish, you'll be in an excellent position to consistently convert live eels to trophy stripers.

CHAPTER EIGHT

RIGGED EELS

By Manny Moreno

My fishing partner, Al Pellini had already landed three nice fish on live eels. I'd had my chances as well but had dropped them all, unable to get solid hook-ups. The early bite ended almost as soon as it started and the fish had completely stopped hitting. It was one of those nights where things started very promising but were now threatening to go wrong. The wind had been calm for days, giving us rare flat seas and allowing us to fish anywhere we wanted. We had set up in the middle of one of our favorite rocky points to start the night's fishing. We figured the fish had moved off and soon it would be time for us to move on as well. Calm nights, like these, gave us the freedom to hunt for fish in all of our favorite spots and explore some new ones. We would take full advantage of it.

Before giving up on this spot, I decided to try one of the two rigged eels I'd packed into my surf bag, mostly as a change from the monotony of the slow retrieve of live eels. Al continued using live eels and I would know if the fish were starting to hit live eels again. It would turn out to be a good controlled experiment. I leaned hard into the next cast knowing that the rigged eel would not tear off the hook like sometimes happens with the live eels. This cast might have gone a bit further but only by a few feet. I let the riggie settle into the water for a moment, allowing it to sink a bit, before starting a slow pumping retrieve. Not expecting much, I was pleasantly surprised when I felt a solid bump on the other end of the line. I tried to convince myself that I had only missed a small fish but at least there were still a few around. My next cast landed in the same area and I had just started the pumping action when a strong hit and solid hook-up interrupted my retrieve. Finally, I was connected to a nice fish that I was confident I would not drop. This bass was no monster but fought very well and turned out to be a very respectable fish in the mid 20s. My world felt right again. Few things make me grumpier than dropping quality bass.

Al Pellini quickly discovered the advantages of fishing with rigged eels.

My next several casts with the rigged eel yielded similar results. I got hits on almost every cast and more often than not follow-up hits if I didn't hook up on the first strike. All the bass were quality fish ranging from the high teens to the high 20s. A half dozen fish quickly turned into a dozen. From my perspective, the bite was really hot but something strange was going on. Al was standing next to me but, since the first few fish, Al had not had another hit on his live eels. The bass were really keying in on my rigged eels. By the time the bite finally ended, I had landed a dozen and a half bass on rigged eels while Al had only managed three more fish on live eels.

Al and I were hard pressed to understand why rigged eels had so drastically out fished the live eels. I have seen rigged eels pick a big fish next to live eels in the past but it had only been one or two fish, which I attributed to coincidence. This was the first time that I'd seen rigged eels completely dominate the action. Other rigged eel experts agree that besides being more efficient, there are many times when rigged eels will out fish live eels. Rigged eels have more and possibly better action than live eels. The keel formed by the two large hooks is the key to the action of the rigged eel and its fish catching ability. Due to this keel, rigged eels swim much more naturally than a live eel on a hook. Trying to impart a live eel with the same kind of action as a rigged eel will cause the live eel to spin making it ineffective.

Although I'd been fishing rigged eels on and off for many years, that night was a turning point in terms of confidence. I had previously caught some good fish and witnessed even better ones, but that night convinced me that the investment in time and effort it takes to rig the eels was well worth it. From that night on, my primary big fish weapon would no longer be live eels. I'd been converted to a rigged eel fisherman. Al was not quite ready to give up his beloved live eels, but he was going to be better prepared the next night.

LEARNING TO RIG

The following afternoon, I found myself conducting a rigging clinic in the parking lot for Al but soon attracted a small crowd of curious passersby. Al had learned his method of rigging eels from his dad while growing up in Rhode Island during the 1950s. Amerigo Pellini had taught Al to rig his eels using a single hook and sometimes added a swim plate. My objective was to teach Al the method of rigging eels using two large Siwash hooks as popularized

Young Al Bentsen holding an impressive 56.4 lbs striper in 1962. The top right corner of the picture shows the rigged eel that seduced the trophy striper.

by some of New York's legendary surf fishermen, most notably Al Bentsen.

In the decade before I was born, Al Bentsen was already refining his rigging techniques and using rigged eels to target big fish. As a young man among veteran fishermen in the early 1950's, Al Bentsen's rigged eels were largely ignored at first. Eventually, rigged eels caught on with his fellow Striper Surf Club members due to their effectiveness with large stripers. Despite the secretive nature of surfcasters, Al Bentsen shared his eel rigging methods with the club, where several members embraced the new technique. Even though they are very effective in catching large stripers, the perceived difficulty of rigging eels coupled with the somewhat messy process has kept rigged eel fishermen to a limited but dedicated number to this day.

Rigged eels are as equally effective in New England as they are in New Jersey.

By the time I joined Striper Surf Club in the late 1980's, interest in rigged eels had declined along with the bass population. A few members still carried on the tradition of rigging eels that Al Bentsen had brought to the club many years before. Much of the credit for what I know about rigged eels and many other aspects of surf fishing goes to my good friend Leif Gobel. Since his days with Striper Surf Club, Leif has taught me and many others eel rigging techniques as passed down to him by senior members of the club. By introducing eel rigging to a number of Long Island surf fishermen, Leif has helped to keep a fishing art form alive.

RIGGING EELS

There are many variations for rigging eels and none are wrong if they catch and hold up well after multiple fish. When rigging eels, the two Siwash hooks are sewn and tied point down into the eel to form a keel that will cause the eel to swim upright enticingly. The keel formed by the two Siwash hooks is vital to the success of the rigged eel and turns the bait into arguably the best bass lure available to surfcasters. If the two hooks are not set securely in place, they stop functioning as a keel and the attraction of the rigged eel diminishes. Once the hooks come loose, the lure is essentially broken and becomes a poorly presented bait. On many occasions, I've found that even during a strong bite, rigged eels stop catching fish once the hooks loosen up. When rigging eels, I try to do the best I can to secure the hooks in place so that they will stand up to many punishing fish without loosening or tearing out of the eels. As I've found deficiencies in my rigging techniques, I've tried to overcome each weakness in order to better hold the keel in place.

While I must admit, it is much easier to learn eel rigging from watching someone else; I will attempt to provide enough details and pictures to provide a thorough overview of the technique. With a little practice, you will be able to become proficient at rigging eels in no time.

CHOOSING RIGGING EELS

Fourteen to eighteen inch eels are the preferred size for rigging. This is one of those times when size does matter. Bigger bass will definitely show a preference for larger eels. With larger eels, many of the smaller fish will fail to get hooked. That is just fine with me. I don't want to waste time and energy fighting and handling small fish when there is a potential for moby bass. Once again, size matters. You'll know you have the right sized eels when you're tackle is straining and it hurts to cast them. The largest bass I ever caught on rigged eel, went for an eel so big I could barely cast it with heavy spinning tackle. Several smaller fish missed getting hooked before the big one finally found it. After two long runs and a clean fight, the big bass pushed my 60 lb hand scale to 53 lbs. I got great satisfaction watching her swim away strongly when I pushed her back into the ocean.

If the eels are not already dead, killing them quickly becomes a necessity. Trying to rig a lively eel is an experience that no one will rush to repeat. While there are many effective ways to kill eels, I prefer to use a copious amount of salt and some ice to keep then cool and wet until dead. Thirty minutes in the lethal mixture should have the eels ready for rigging. Previously dead or even previously frozen eels will work nearly as well, although they are not quite as firm. Fresh rigged eels will hold up better during fishing and last longer.

PREPPING THE HOOKS

The Mustad 9510XXXDT Siwash hooks in 8/0 and 9/0 sizes are my preferred hooks for rigging. For most eels and fishing locations, I rig my eels with 8/0 hooks. For bigger eels or times when I want one to sink faster, I will go with 9/0 hooks. Eels rigged with 9/0 hooks are much more likely to get stuck on the bottom on rocky beaches where I do most of my fishing. Other hooks of similar size and shape may also work well but I have not found a reason to try them. Mustad Siwash hooks come with open eyes so a little prep work will be required to get them ready. I like to close the eye of the hook as much as I can manage with a sturdy pair of

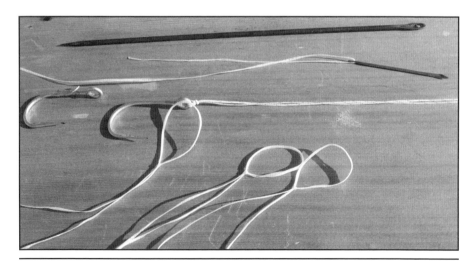

pliers. I was never able to close the eyes to my satisfaction, but this problem went away when I started to solder the eyes closed.

On the front or head hook, I attach a three quarter inch long piece of thick copper wire to the outside of the hook shank a half inch from the eye to form a reverse barb that will anchor the head of the eel onto the hook. The reverse barb was a modification developed by John Papciak to solve the problem of the head hook twisting around as the eel loosened up. In John's original design, the wire barb was wrapped on with thread and glued using epoxy. Scott Hayes, always handy with tools, took John's idea one step further and used solder to attach the barb much more permanently. I owe a great deal of credit to both John and Scott for helping me refine my rigging techniques and develop confidence in fishing with rigged eels.

To attach the reverse barb, hold the hook in a vise while using a pair of vise grips to hold the wire barb in place until the solder makes the connection permanent. Once you get the hang of it, an hour or two will be enough time to prepare enough hooks to last a full season. My final step in hook preparation is to sharpen the hooks using a file.

MATERIAL

The other materials you will need include a thirty inch piece of 50# Dacron, a twelve inch rigging needle, a heavy curved sewing needle, some waxed rigging floss and a pair of scissors for trimming excess line.

STEP 1 – PREP THE EEL

Using paper towels, remove as much of the slime as possible from the length of the eel. The eels should be stretched out and loosened up until supple. "Breaking" the tail vertebrae for added action is recommended by many riggers though I have never found it to make a difference. Others have told me that breaking the vertebrae weakens the eel causing it to fall apart faster. You decide what works best for you.

STEP 2 – PREP THE TAIL HOOK

Fold the Dacron in half and tie the loop end to the rear hook using a Palomar knot. The tag ends of the knot will be used to connect the rear hook to the head hook. When tied properly, each tag end of the knot will have equal strength in case one side should fail or get bitten by a bluefish. Taken together, they will have nearly 100 lbs of breaking strength with zero stretch.

STEP 3 – INSERT TAIL HOOK

Thread the double tag end of the Dacron line through the eye of the rigging needle. Insert the rigging needle through the vent of the eel, threading through the eel and out of the mouth. Pull the end of the Dacron out of the eel's mouth while inserting the eye of the rear hook into the eel's vent. It helps to lay the eel flat and press the eye of the hook down into the vent.

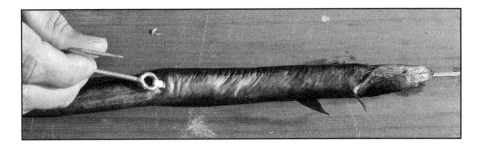

STEP 4 – INSERT HEAD HOOK

Before inserting the head hook into the eel, carefully calculate the placement of the hook. The point of the hook should be centered in the bottom of the throat of the eel while the lips of the eel should close around the base of the eye. Once you are satisfied with the position of the head hook, thread the Dacron through the eye of the hook. This is where having the eye of the hook soldered closed really helps because there is no gap on the eye for the Dacron to slip into. Stretch the tag line from the rear to head hooks until both are in the desired position and secure the head hook with a half hitch. Double check the hook placements and adjust the half hitch as necessary. The Dacron line should be stretched but not overly taught. If the line is too tight, the eel will be kinked and not swim properly. If there is slack line, the rear hook will tear out when a fish hits it. When both hooks are in the desired position, secure the head hook with a few additional half hitches and two sets of square knots on opposite sides. You will need to pull the hook shank out a half inch or so to complete the knots then push the hook shank with knots back in.

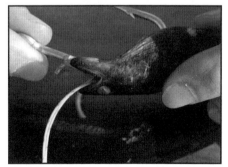

STEP 5 – SECURE HEAD HOOK

Using the rigging floss, prepare two or three sets of double loop slip knots. Push the reverse barb into the center of the inside of the head of the eel. Secure the head hook with the slip knots by placing loops around the head of the eel in front and behind the reverse barb. Pulling the tag ends of the slip knot in opposite directions will help cinch it tightly. The slip knots should be secured in place using three or four sets of square knots on alternating sides. A third slip knot may be required on the head of larger eels.

STEP 6 – SECURE TAIL HOOK

Using a curved sewing needle and a fifteen inch length of rigging floss, sew the rear hook into place by stitching figure eights into the middle of the bottom of the eel, through the eye of the hook and out of the side of the eel. The stitch should exit the eel in the vicinity of the line between the pale lower half and the dark upper half. The next stitch should enter the same hole on the bottom of the eel and exit on the opposite side. After about three or four stitches on each side, use a square knot to lock the stitches. With the remaining ends of the floss, tie three or four alternating square knots around the entire eel. This area of the rigged eel tends to be one of the first to fail. By reinforcing it with extra knots around the eel, the rear hook will remain securely in place. As a final step, add a slip loop around the shank of the rear hook and lock with a few square knots to help prevent the stitches from tearing.

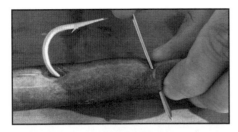

Your eels are now ready to go fishing. With a little practice, you should be able to rig three or four eels within an hour.

STORAGE

Assuming you are not going fishing right away, you will need to store your rigged eels until you are ready to hit the water. I like to neatly stack two or three rigged eels in a ziplock freezer bag and store the bag in a small cooler, well iced. For longer term storage, I freeze the eels in the ziplock bags. If I remember, I will add some coarse salt to the eels prior to freezing. The rigged eels that survive a night's fishing can be refrozen several times before they become too mushy for any more trips to the beach. Old mushy eels will catch fish, but they won't hold up very well and will tear apart fairly easily. As long as there are no pesky bluefish around to chop up your eels, a well rigged fresh eel can last many trips. Usually you can catch four to six fish per rigged eel before it begins to fall apart but I've gotten as many as nineteen bass on a single rigged eel.

There are a few logistical advantages to rigged eels over live eels. For starters, you don't have to work to keep rigged eels alive. With proper care, rigged eels can be stored a long time and will always be on hand when its time to go fishing. During multi-day fishing trips, a cooler with some ice is all you need to keep your rigged eels in good condition.

For a night on the beach, I pack a couple of ziplock bags with two or three rigged eels each and carry them in a belt pouch or surf bag. The Aquaskinz single row surf bag is perfect for carrying rigged eels and an adequate selection of plugs. The pouch on the front of the bag will hold a good number of rigged eels along with a few rigged sluggos, bucktails, shads and anything else needed for a night of fishing. The safety clip will insure that you don't lose any of the prized eels you worked so diligently to rig. I also carry a handful of waxed thread slip loops for on the water emergency repairs. Sometimes, a slip loop and a few knots is all it takes to restore an eel to its former fish-catching glory.

TACKLE

I cannot stress enough how important every aspect of the equipment is. I pay strict attention to every facet regardless of how trivial it might seem. When it comes to fishing, I want the best, strongest, most dependable equipment and always make sure that it is well maintained and ready to go. For rigged eels, I favor a medium action custom ten foot graphite rod, built from either a Kennedy Fischer or Lamiglas blank. I find lighter rods do not have the power to throw a heavy rigged eel or drive in those big Siwash hooks.

This rod is well matched by a Van Staal VS300 or VS250 surf reel. Either reel will do the job well but it's hard to beat the VS300 for cranking power. Also, I find the drag is smoother on the VS300 when tangling with big fish. When targeting large stripers with rigged eels, a Kennedy Fischer rod with a VS300 is my primary outfit. On nights when I plan to throw a bit more variety, such as switching from rigged eels to plugs to plastics to bucktails, I will opt for one of the sticks with a VS250. The lighter reel is a better match for tossing smaller offerings but still has plenty of power for fighting large fish.

All of my surf reels have the drag clicker removed so as to not wake up the neighbors when a fish runs. I service the drags with Shimano drag lube. This keeps the drags silky smooth in spite of the frequent submerging my reels are likely to endure. I don't care for extra features on my reels that are likely to fail at the worst possible moment. Keeping everything as simple as possible allows me to focus on fishing, not on tackle. Added complexity should only be considered if it provides a significant advantage. Van Staal reels nicely satisfy my need for durable, low maintenance, simple to use reels.

LINE

In the last few years, I've settled on using Spiderwire Stealth in 50 lb test for all of my rigged eel fishing. Periodically as new products come around, I give something else a try but end up disappointed and go back to using Spiderwire. Along with casting well, this line has extremely good abrasion resistance. You never know when you're going to need it. A couple of years ago, a truly big bass headed for a distant rock after a long

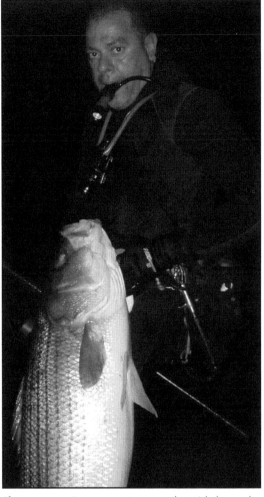

If you are going to cast your eel amid the rocks, make sure you use a line that has good abrasion resistance.

run. The location of the rock was clearly defined by large boils whenever a good swell went past. Failing to turn the fish as it headed around the structure, I eased up on the drag and applied gentle but steady pressure hoping to get the fish to come back around. Eventually the fish came out of the rocks but I was now concerned about the condition of the line. The line held up very nicely and I managed to land my best bass of the year, just two pounds shy of fifty pounds. Needing to pull big fish out of rocks seems to happen to me a couple times each year. Spiderwire Stealth has not failed me yet when it comes to fishing with rigged eels in rocky beaches.

LEADERS

My typical leader when fishing for striped bass used to be a three and a half foot length of 60 to 80 lbs monofilament leader with a barrel swivel tied to one end using an improved clinch knot and a #54 Coastlock snap tied to the other. When I started fishing with rigged eels, I was quickly forced to re-think my long-standing terminal tackle philosophy. Through the experience of losing some very big fish, I've come to the conclusion that getting rid of the snap and tying the rigged eel directly to the business end of the leader is an absolute requirement.

Bass are able to leverage or bite open the snaps attached to large Siwash hooks. I don't know how it happened but I clearly remember the first time. I had been fishing a long night in a big fish spot with nothing to show for it. Suddenly, on a cast to the right, I got a solid hit. As I quickly leaned back to set the hook, I could tell it was a good fish. The fish shook its head for a moment then slowly started taking line with deep tail pumps. All of a sudden, for no reason that I could determine, plink, the fish was gone. With no resistance coming from the other end of the line, I could only surmise that the fish had somehow broken the line. As I retrieved the slack line, the swivel bumped into the rod tip confusing me further. Had the fish broken my leader? Further inspection revealed the sad truth. My line, swivel and leader were intact. My snap had been straightened open. I figured this was just a rare incident as snaps occasionally open with other lures but I was to be taught differently, the hard way.

One experience like this should have been enough but sometimes I need repeated lessons to get the message. On a couple of other occasions, I've been the unfortunate student of this tough lesson, losing quality fish to failed snaps. I don't blame the snap or the manufacturers. These snaps have worked just fine for plugs and bucktails, even under the significant pressure of fishing inlets and heavy currents. My theory is that fish are able to use the thick wire of the large Siwash hook to twist and pop open the snap. Once the snap is open, the battle is lost, along with a good fish and a meticulously rigged eel.

When I'm fishing rigged eels these days, I start with a four foot leader connected to the main line with a quality swivel. The other end I tie directly to the head hook of the rigged eel using an improved clinch knot.

Since there is no snap, the leaders are a very simple affair. I trim back the leader as necessary to change rigged eels, try some plugs or just cut back the leader as it gets scraped. As the leader gets shortened down to less than three feet, it is time to put on a fresh one.

I am not a big fan of fluorocarbon leader material. I have found fluorocarbon to be brittle and not

With rigged eels, you can productively cover much more water then with live eels by varying your retrieve.

worth the extra cost. Instead, I prefer to use quality monofilament leader material. On nights when the fishing is slow and I want to reduce the visibility of the leader, I will tie the rigged eel directly to the 50# braid using a Palomar knot. Tying directly has rewarded me with some very good fish on nights when I've found the fish to be leader shy. Without a leader to grab, extra care must be taken when landing fish.

FISHING WITH RIGGED EELS

Anyone used to fishing with live eels will need to adjust their techniques in order to be successful with rigged eels. One of the reasons I switched from live to rigged eels is that I had gotten bored with the monotonously slow retrieve of fishing with live eels. Rigged eels require a higher level of active participation from the fisherman. The caster imparts action onto the rigged eels through a variety of retrieves and speeds. My typical approach is to cast the eel, let it settle and sink to some desired depth, then start a slow retrieve with a periodic pump or twitch of the rod. The speed of the retrieve and rhythm of the rod pumps can be varied to alter the eel's action. When the action is slow, I try different retrieves looking for some combination that will entice fish to strike.

With rigged eels, I feel I am able to productively cover much more of the water column than with live eels. Rigged eels can be worked as soon as they hit the water or allowed to sink to different depths. Slowing or speeding the retrieve will swim the riggie through different depths of the water column. I've had fish hit right on top on a faster moving rigged eel, but most of the time I try to get the rigged eel closer to the bottom, particularly in fast moving currents.

Because I generally work the rigged eel faster than a live eel, I am able to cover more water faster. When I have room and conditions allow, I constantly fan cast to cover a wider area side to side. Many times, there is a sweet spot where most of the fish are holding. Once I locate or get to know the hot spot, I tend to concentrate my efforts in that area. I will periodically fan the casts to other areas if the usual hot spot is not producing.

Bass will often strike the eel just after the rod pump. The strikes will feel much more solid than hits on live eels. Because there is less slack in the line when fishing with rigged eels, some of the hits will be absolutely crushing. As opposed to live eels, fisherman should set-up immediately and firmly when getting a hit on rigged eels. Most of the time, the fish will hit the front hook but there will be plenty of fish hooked on the rear hook.

A sturdy rod and a tight drag will be required to drive the large Siwash hooks in. I often set up a second time if I didn't feel a solid enough hook-up the first time. Once those big hooks get a good bite into a fish, they rarely come off. Most of the fish will be firmly hooked in the jaw. Because you will be setting up immediately, rarely will you get any deep or gut-hooked fish. With rigged eels, you will be able to release most of the big ones in good shape to fight another day.

LOCATIONS

Most of my rigged eel fishing takes place on rocky beaches where I feel my chances for a big fish are significantly improved. On a recent trip to one of our favorite rocky beaches, the wind had come around hard from the east during the day. Usually, when fishing with rigged eels, I prefer to have the wind at my back but there was no way to escape the strong cross wind along the south facing shoreline. Without a tail wind to help extend our casting distance, we would need to adjust our approach if we hoped to reach productive waters. Strikes can sometimes occur quite close, but getting the rigged eels out into deeper water increases the chances of encountering trophy stripers. The best we could hope for this night was getting out on the sides of the rocky points and using the crosswind to fish into the deeper water of the coves.

I let Al take the lead rock, thinking his live eels would need all the help they could get to reach the fish in the strong cross wind. I set up on a rock directly behind him, which normally would have been a problem for casting. However, tonight we were going to fish sideways and use the strong wind to some advantage. Our first casts confirmed that we had chosen well. We immediately connected with bass in the mid to high 20s. Subsequent casts yielded a few more fish as the steady bite turned into a

Even during the height of summer, stripers are caught by dedicated fisherman willing to fish rigged eels deep into the night.

slow pick of quality stripers up to 35 lbs. The strong cross wind might have prevented us reaching good water where larger fish are often lurking but by finding a way to get some wind at our backs and taking advantage of what the structure offered, we had managed to find some very good fishing. We don't often get ideal conditions for preferred locations but by adjusting our approach to suit the conditions we can sometimes locate a few quality stripers.

There are many surf fishing areas that can produce quality fish on a regular basis, but big fish spots generally have a few things in common: structure, current and close proximity to deeper water. Large stripers do not spend much of their time in shallow near shore water, but they will often come close to shore to feed. Whether you're fishing sandy or rocky beaches, off ocean jetties or in protected bays, look for underwater structure such as bars, points, coves or deep holes that create transition zones. Marine life will congregate along changes in underwater terrain and those zones will be key staging areas for large stripers. Through trial and error, some experience and a bit of luck, you will eventually figure out where to fish rigged eels productively along your favorite beaches. By fishing with rigged eels around good structure, it will be only a matter of time before you encounter a trophy striper.

WHEN TO FISH RIGGED EELS

After you've figured out how to rigged your eels perfectly and found the best structure in your area, you still won't catch fish unless you are fishing at the right time. Regardless of your technique, you can't catch what isn't around. Predicting the arrival and peak periods of fishing for large stripers is a combination of art and science. Along with years of experience, I rely on personal fishing logs and fishing reports to give me a good idea of when to expect large stripers to be around. Large bass will return to the same locations every year, often within the same week they did the previous year.

I start hearing about reports of big fish being caught in New Jersey in April and May. In my home waters off Long Island, good numbers of large stripers start arriving in May, with June having solid action. In Rhode Island, June is a good month with solid fishing lasting into July. The same timeframe applies to Massachusetts, adjusting the dates later as the fish migrate north. The migration pattern will reverse itself starting in August in northern areas and progressing later into the year as the fish find their way south again. During the north and south migrations, there is a two to four week peak period when the main body of big fish will pass through any given area. Fish rigged eels often during that peak period and you will be rewarded with a trophy bass or two.

Even during the height of summer, stripers are caught by dedicated fisherman willing to fish rigged eels deep into the night. The summer "doldrums" will usually produce fewer fish but can sometimes produce a resident trophy striper.

Weather is the unpredictable variable thrown into the predictability of the migration pattern. Storms and water temperatures can accelerate or delay the arrival of fish. The same weather will affect the movement of bait concentrations. Once the big stripers arrive, the right weather pattern is needed to bring them near shore. Finding areas that are productive during prevailing conditions will be the key to consistent success.

The leading edges of the storms can spur good fishing in many areas. But finding areas that are fishable with rigged eels can be a challenge. High winds and big seas can render open waters impossible to fish with rigged eels. That is a good time to fish sheltered waters inside inlets and bays. As the weather settles and wave heights diminish, there is often a good opportunity for large stripers.

STRIPER MOONS

In case I have not been clear on this yet, rigged eels are for fishing at night. Ideally, the moon and the stars will be the only sources of light. Boat fishermen often talk about the full moon as the bass moon but for surf men, the real bass moon is the new moon. As far as I'm concerned, it can never be too dark for bass. Even on the most remote beaches, you will still have the moon, the stars and often other sources of ambient light. Although I've caught some very nice bass on rigged eels during full moons, the majority of the time I prefer fishing darker nights.

Bluefish, which are particularly active during bright moon periods, are the bane of all rigged eel fishermen. Few things are more aggravating than to toss out a rigged eel that you proudly tied and sewed to perfection, only to have a toothy blue varmint come along and chop off the tail, rendering the eel almost useless on the very first cast. Most of the time, they don't even give you the courtesy of getting hooked, so you can get even. If too many bluefish are around, switch to plugs or at the very least, live eels, though losing live eels to bluefish is only slightly more palatable than losing rigged eels.

While most of my fishing trips are planned around the dark moon periods, the full or bright moon periods will yield some very good fish as well if you can find waters that are not completely infested by bluefish. If you do manage to evade the blues, some very good fishing can be found even on the brightest moons by altering your approach. Deep waters, such as around inlets, help to diminish the effects of bright moons. I can recall a few full moon nights when the bass ate rigged eels like they were going out of style.

When hit by the bright light of the moon, leaders can resemble optic fibers, radiating with light. Stripers, particularly large ones, can sometimes become quite leader shy. If action is slow, this would be a good time to ditch the leaders. But tying rigged eels directly to braid poses some added challenges. Care must be taken when landing nice fish since braid will easily slice hands and fingers if one is not careful. Also, there is the added chance of a fish cutting the line on some structure, but I have not had this happen with 50 lb braid. By eliminating the leaders, I have been rewarded with a number of 30 and 40 lb class stripers when fish were just not hitting rigs with leaders. With a few adjustments, even the brightest moon periods can yield some extraordinary catches.

TIME TO GO FISHING

I hope that I have been able to entertain while providing you with enough useful information to get started fishing with rigged eels. Once you develop a bit of skill and confidence, you will be convinced that fishing with rigged eels is one of the most productive and exciting methods for targeting large stripers. Follow the migration patterns, fish around the big fish structure with rigged eels and strong tackle and you will be rewarded with a trophy striper. A hand scale and a waterproof camera are all you need to record your trophy catch while doing your part to maintain a healthy population of cow stripers.

CHAPTER NINE

SLUG-GO:
A LIVE EEL ALTERNATIVE

By Steve McKenna

I started surf fishing for striped bass in 1973. Soon after my initial introduction to surf casting, for bass, I quickly learned of the productivity of the use of live and rigged eels for this species. Some of my earliest surf-fishing mentors like "Gill" Gliottone, Matt Squillante, Andy Lemar and Frank Benassi touted the importance of utilizing eels if I wanted to score consistently with stripers of all sizes. They were right! Casting an eel, either live or rigged, into productive waters was almost automatic.

Over the 30 seasons since my rookie year, I have racked up some impressive scores on live or rigged eels. Notably, the 48-½ pounder (my second largest surf bass) taken on a live eel at Gooseberry Island, Westport, MA. On a cold Halloween night; two consecutive 800 pound nights at the Chatham (MA) inlet in the early 90's on rigged eels; six 40 7great full moon evening with live eels at the Mussel Bed (RI) with a 40 and 42 lb fish; a 41 and 47 pounder at the mouth of Narrow River (RI) on rigged eels one election night not too long ago; and on and on and on...

Live or rigged eels were the best bait for stripers in my book and other than the early spring, I rarely fished without them until three seasons ago. In the summer of 2003 two of my long time surf-fishing friends, Tim Coleman, former editor of The New England Fisherman magazine and Pat Abate, owner of Rivers End Tackle Shop in Old Saybrook, CT. formally introduced me to a soft plastic artificial bait that they had been using with amazing success for striped bass. Both of these gentlemen are sharpies, consummate surfcasters with about seventy plus years experience chasing linesiders from shore. Both men have a penchant for consistently landing real bass. Moreover, Tim and Pat were always strong advocates of live or rigged eels.

The soft plastic bait they have become so excited about was the 9" Slug-Go manufactured by Herb Reed's Lunker City Company in nearby Meridan, Connecticut. Tim and Pat were so impressed with the Slug-Go that they have just about shunned eels in favor of this amazing rubber creation. Furthermore, both Coleman and Abate cited numerous surf-fishing trips in the past when the use of the 9" Slug-Go resulted in some unbelievable striper catches. In fact, Tim and Pat have both exceeded the magic forty pounds mark with this artificial within the last few seasons.

At first I was extremely skeptical of this artificial alternative to the eel. I never believed that the Slug-Go could come close to replacing the real thing. My feelings changed dramatically however when I had the opportunity to see, first hand, the 9" Slug-Go in action. On several occasions I fished with Tim and Pat, I using my beloved eels and they the 9" Slug-Go. Amazingly our catches were similar and on more than one occasion they out fished me. Observing their comparative and sometimes better success, I decided to give the Slug-Go a try. After a bit of experimentation and some impressive action during the last three seasons, I am now a true believer of the Slug-Go's fish catching abilities. I have not bought a live eel since the summer of 2003! I have taken small bass, big bass and a lot of bass. My most recent was a 30-pound fish taken three nights before writing this article. My most memorable night in the surf however using this fantastic artificial had to be last year. It was late September and I was on my way to Cuttyhunk Island, Massachusetts for my first surf-fishing

Targeting big stripers by casting Slug-go's in between boulders is a very productive technique along the entire striper coast.

endeavor on that piece of real estate. After scouting the island's shoreline by foot during daytime hours I decided to surf fish the southwest side of Cutty's shores that coming evening.

About seven in the evening I made my way to the selected southwest side with high hopes of catching some quality stripers. I had heard only good things about this storied place and its unbelievable bass surf action. Just before dark I clipped on a 9" white (albino shad) rigged Slug-Go and cast it in between the southwest corner's boulders. On about my tenth flip of the Slug-Go I hooked and landed a small striper. My next cast produced another bass of similar size. This was definitely a very good sign but even better was the small bait that I had observed spraying in amongst the rocks and surf line in front of me while catching these pint size linesiders. My excitement continued to build anticipating that bigger fish might move in after dark because of all the bait.

As darkness fell I took off the white Slug-Go and replaced it with a 9" all black model and began working the water in front of me. It was a perfect night to surf fish, a light southwest wind pushing just enough swell and water directly in my face. On top of that, a recent new moon made for a very dark night, which I prefer and said moon made for higher tides and stronger rips. The tide was high and falling and the presence of baitfish rounded out ideal surf-fishing conditions.

The first hit came about five minutes after dark. It was one of those smashing strikes, the kind that almost pulls the rod out of your hands. Approximately 10 minutes later after a nice battle with some very strong and sustained runs a striper about 35 lbs. lay at my feet, spent from the fight. Not having a hand scale with me I could only measure this fish – 45" – before releasing it. This fish chewed up my Slug-Go, which is unfortunately one of the only drawbacks of this rubber bait, so I quickly snapped on a fresh one and began casting again.

Within minutes I had another smashing hit and hooked up with another powerful bass. This striper was a clone of my first big fish – 44 ½ inches with a healthy girth. This fish was quickly released. I changed the mangled Slug-Go and began casting. The next fish hit about two minutes later. Same great battle, same size fish, same chewed up Slug-Go and same release... this scenario was repeated another 30 times over the next

3 hours or so. Unbelievably, the first 10 fish I landed were in that 45 inch range going about 35 lbs. The smallest bass taken in this blitz was 12 pounds. All fish were released except one, which I kept for the grill. It weighed 37 ½ pounds. All 33 stripers were taken on the 9" black modified Slug-Go. On that most unforgettable evening I went through all 24 pre rigged Slug-Go's that were in my surf bag. I don't believe that I would have done any better with live or rigged eels that night, and I also know from experience that other artificials would not have worked nearly as well as the Slug-Go. Specifically, over the last several seasons I have conducted informal experiments with my hybrid Slug-Go and other proven striper killers, such as needle fish, metal lip swimmers, plastic swimmers and other soft rubber/plastic baits. The modified Slug-Go out fished these other fakes time after time. I purposely changed from the Slug-Go to another lure while into fish. The results were always in favor of the Slug-Go. So, while some may scoff at the notion, I can say without hesitation that the 9-inch Slug-Go is as effective as a live or rigged eel and other striper artificials.

RIGGING THE 9" SLUG-GO

As previously mentioned in the article I have done some experimenting with the 9" Slug-Go before perfecting it into a striper catching machine. The following is a list of materials needed to modify this bait so the angler will achieve optimum results.

MATERIALS REQUIRED;

• 9" Slug-Gos

• Rigging needle, which can be easily fashioned from the bottom section of a wire coat hanger. Cut 10" section from bottom of thin wire coat hangers sharpen on end to a point and, with a pair of pliers, bend other end to a small u-shape hook

• 7/0 Gamakatsu hooks either live bait or octopus models (these hooks work the best. They are extremely sharp, strong and don't rust quickly. However, an angler can use other comparable hooks if desired)

• 50lb test Dacron line by Cortland

- Super Glue or Zap-a-Gap glue or any quick drying, strong cement.
- Herb Reed/Lunker City Slug-Go insert weights – Size 3/32 oz

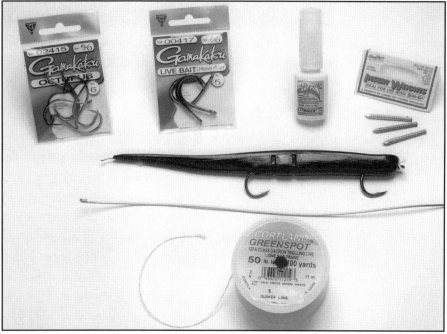

The materials needed to rig a 9" Slug-Go: 5/0 and 7/0 Gamakatsu hooks, Zap A Gap Glue, Herb Reed insert weights, size 3/32 oz., a rigging needle and 50 pound test Cortland Dacron line.

RIGGING PROCESS

Step One: Double 24" of 50lb Dacron line tying tag ends with an over hand knot.

Step Two: Tie looped end of doubled Dacron to 7/0 Gamakastu hook with an improved clinch knot.

Step Three: Attach doubled Dacron line to u-shape hook on the rigging needle

Step Four: Insert pointed end of rigging needle into the body of the Slug-Go just south of the segmentation section in the middle of the bait.

Step Five: Push rigging needle thru the center of the Slug-Go exiting out the front of the lure head. Then pull the rigging needle, Dacron line and hook thru the rest of the Slug-Go until 7/0 hook is snugged up into the body of the lure.

Step Six: Insert 7/0 hook half way into the head of the Slug-Go. Then half-hitch doubled Dacron line up the exposed shank of head hook. Make an over hand knot after the half hitches are completed. This will prevent half hitches from unraveling.

Step Seven: Liberally coat half hitched Dacron with glue then push tie 7/0 hook into the head of the Slug-Go.

Step Eight: After glue dries, push one Slug-Go insert weight directly into the tail of the lure and another weight on either side of the Slug-Go behind the head hook parallel to the body. If more weight is needed say due to wind, deeper water or strong rip currents don't be afraid to add another insert weight parallel to the other two head area weights. The addition of a fourth weight will not foul up the action of this lure and it will make it much more versatile.

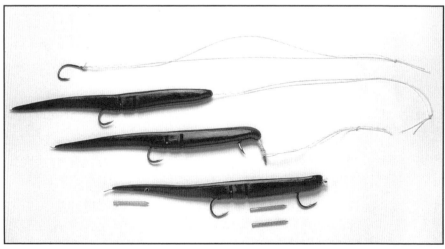

The rigging process. See article for details.

When the 9" Slug-Go is prepared in this fashion it casts well, has much better action than the un-weighted Slug-Go, hooks more fish that "short hit" the lure and enables the angler to fish all water depths and rips.

FISHING THE SLUG-GO

The modified Slug-Go should be fished much like a Zara Spook or Pencil Popper lure. The surf caster must use a moderate retrieve twitching the rod quickly throughout and keeping the lure subsurface at all times, which is important. It has been my experience that stripers, particularly big bass really prefer a subsurface presentation of the rubber artificial, even if only inches under the surface after dark. During the day, bass will most always pounce on a Slug-Go on the surface but after the sun goes down it is a very different story. Keeping the Slug-Go under the surface can be achieved by holding your rod parallel to the water and to the side of your body throughout the retrieve. In deeper water or rip currents allow the Slug-Go to sink a bit and count the seconds as it sinks. Try starting your retrieve after it has sunk for a specific number of seconds, and when you get a hit, allow the lure to sink to that level on subsequent casts. Vary the amount of time you allow it to drop until you find the prime-feeding zone. That brings me to another drawback of using the Slug-Go. As previously mentioned in this chapter, the modified Slug-Go is not very durable. A striped bass, even a small one can tear apart this soft rubber bait easily. Generally, only one fish, maybe two can be caught on the lure. This is why carrying several pre-rigged lures is highly recommended. I usually tote a dozen or so in my surf bag. Incidentally, I have found that the medium sized surf bag made by Aquaskinz Co. of New York, ideal for carrying these artificials. A dozen pre rigged Slug-Go's can be stored lengthwise in the front pocket of said bag. I was going to say that one of the other failings of my Slug-Go is its inability to work well in very deep water – over 10 feet – or in very deep swift moving current similar to those conditions found at the Cape Cod Canal in Massachusetts or other deep water inlets all along our striper coast. My altered Slug-Go just is not effective in these locations primarily because it will not sink fast enough. Unfortunately, my Slug-Go is a shallow water lure, which is most effective in, water less than 10 feet, with moderately rough surf and minimal current. When fishing deeper and fast moving seas some surf men utilize a lead headed jig on the front of the Slug-Go. I personally know some Cape Cod Canal surf fishermen who employ such a technique and do very well. But remember, when a jig head is used on a 9" Slug-Go

the action changes dramatically and is totally different than my version of the Slug-Go. I have been and will continue to experiment with different weighting scenarios with my style of the Slug-Go so as to maintain the desired action. I experiment because I want to be able to sustain the action in deep water and strong current locations. The action is what I feel is the most important and main attraction of the lure for big stripers.

Steve's favorite set-up for working Slug-go's is an 8 or 9-foot fiberglass rod, and a 20-pound Ande Back Country monofilament line spooled on a quality reel.

DO NOT fish this lure like a live eel or at a slow pace. I firmly believe the Slug-Go's appeal to stripers is its erratic action and said action can only be achieved by fishing the lure as stated. Furthermore, when the fish hits the lure set up immediately much like any other artificial. Tackle needed to fish this lure can be the surfcaster's choice. However, I like to use a rod between 8 and 9 feet long. The shorter rod helps me stay in contact with the Slug-Go. Shorter surf sticks also are more user friendly while putting the rigged and weighted Slug-Go thru its paces. Longer rods of 10 to 11 feet become too heavy and too unwieldy especially when the rod is placed at the anglers side during the second part of the retrieve. Don't be afraid of whipping bigger stripers or with casting distance with shorter surf sticks. I find that I can easily reach, fight and land big bass on 8 or 9-foot rods. The following three surf rods that I use specifically for the Slug-Go have

enabled me to land a lot of 30 to 41 lb. bass. I like rods made by the Star Rod Company of Morehead City, North Carolina. My favorites are the 8-foot – Deluxe DLX 15 -8ct and the Deluxe-DLX-25 which is believe it or not 7 feet 6 inches. Both rods are fiberglass, which I firmly believe, beats a fish much faster and more efficiently than graphite. Moreover, both rods cast the rigged and weighted Slug-Go like a dream. I have caught a lot of 30 to 40 lb. fish on both outfits.

The third favorite is another fiberglass model. This rod is a custom made by Wickford Rod Works in North Kingstown R.I. Bob at Wickford Rod Works fashions a great Slug-Go stick from a BT-108 3m Lamiglas Blank. The only modification to this blank is two inches are cut off the tip. The finished rod is 8 feet 10 inches overall, throws a weighted, two hook Slug-Go a mile and will take on the biggest striper the surf has to offer. On these spinning sticks I am very lucky to be able to use and afford reels by Van Staal of

One of the many quality stripers Steve has caught on a Slug-go lure.

Tulsa, Oklahoma. I really like the VS200 model on all of the aforementioned sticks. If you can't afford a Van Staal I would go with a comparable sized Penn Quantum, Shimano or Daiwa Reel. Spend the most you can on a reel. A quality reel with a good drag that is durable is important while surfcasting for trophy bass. I load these fine reels with my favorite striper line, 20-pound Ande Back Country monofilament. I like Ande because it is very strong, castable and very abrasion resistant which is imperative because most of my surf fishing is around rocks.

I'm not a fan of braided line because it self destructs around rocks but if I had to choose one for casting Slug-Gos in the surf it would be one of the more popular brands like Suffix, Power Pro or Fire Line in 40 or 50 pound test strengths. One last note on gear to throw the Slug-Gos, I would recommend staying away from conventional rods and reels. With conventional outfits the correct action is harder to achieve which is all-important when fishing with this artificial. Do yourself a favor, stick with spinning tackle when surf casting the modified Slug-Go. I always use a fluorocarbon leader with a quality ball bearing swivel and snap because I like to be as stealthy as possible and fishing the Slug-Go does cause line twist without the ball bearing hardware. My favorite fluorocarbon leader material is offered by the Orvis Co. of Vermont. It is called Mirage and I like the 60 lb. test strength. This stuff is very, very abrasive resistant which comes in handy when a large striper tries to rub you off on submerged boulders. I make my leaders longer, about 4 feet with a top quality ball bearing swivel at one end in the 150 to 200 lb. strength and a breakaway snap at the other end. The large ball bearing swivel prevents line twist, which is common when fishing the Slug-Go in the aforementioned manner. The F-11 breakaway snap makes changing the Slug-Gos a snap and it is super strong.

Color is the next thing you will have to consider. Herb Reed makes Slug-Go's in a wide variety of shades. I have tried them all but all black is by far my favorite. It works the best during low light periods and after dark. Black sparkle or rainbow trout colors would be my next choices if I couldn't find black. I don't fish much during the day but a charter captain friend of mine, Jimmy White, who guides anglers in sunlight and who is very familiar with the productivity of soft plastics, prefers all white and pink (bubblegum) Slug-Go's. Captain White has taken fish into the 40's on these colors. As mentioned, I don't fish much during daylight hours because big striped bass are decidedly nocturnal particularly for the surfcaster. I do make some exceptions to that rule fishing daytime in the month of May into early June on occasion. When I go out in sunlight during that period I will always use white or pink Slug-Go's because during May and June Rhode Island has a great squid run and these colors appropriately mimic the squid. Sometimes some very large bass can be fooled by the Slug-Go in daylight when the squid are thick.

The 9" Slug-Go is absolutely the best artificial I have ever used during my long career pursuing stripers in the surf. When I cast this lure into productive water along any coastline I am sure that a bass will take the Slug-Go if they are present – Just like the confidence I had when I fished with live or rigged eels.

CHAPTER TEN

EEL SKIN LURES

By Zeno Hromin

Eel skin lures have caught a disproportionate number of large striped bass over the years when compared to plain wood or plastic lures. Yet, for some reason, they have lost much of their popularity over the last few decades. Some think that this is due to the current craze over collecting "custom" wood lures. However, I think that it has to do with the unwillingness of the current generation of surfcasters to get their hands dirty. Let's face it; we live in a society in which we have little precious "free" time. We drive our kids from one organized activity to another. We have household chores and a million other things that take up our free time. Dealing with procuring, skinning and rigging an eel skin on a lure takes time and effort. It is then not surprising, that when we go fishing, all we want to do is grab our surf bag and hit the beach.

But hunting for big stripers requires a different mindset and level of preparedness than just "fishing" does. Yes, it requires some hard and unpleasant chores in order to give us the best possible chance of tangling with that fish of our dreams. Eel skin lures offer us a shortcut in our pursuit of large stripers. I readily concede that most of the time live and rigged eels will out-fish plugs fitted with eel skins. However, fishing with live or rigged eels requires certain conditions to be present in the surf. They often are ineffective during periods of strong onshore wind, as they cast like a wet rag. During periods when current is moving fast, it is difficult to get live or rigged eels deep in the water column, where they can be most productive. Eel skin plugs however, are not limited by these factors. In fact, some of them really come into their own under these conditions, as we are able to make adjustments to our lure, to compensate for fast currents.

Needlefish in particular can be used to punch through a strong wind with ease, reaching well beyond where a live or rigged eel can, even under optimal conditions. This alone should be enough to motivate you to add an eel skin to your favorite lure. However, if you are still not sold on it, I can tell you about a few more wonderful attributes. Once rigged onto a lure, just rinsing the lure in fresh water and storing it in a freezer will easily maintain the eel skin. This is why I said that eel skin plugs are in a way a shortcut for a surfcaster who wants all the benefits of fishing with a rigged or live eel, but does not want to be bothered with rigging needles or live snakes. The reason for rinsing is not to prolong the durability of the skin, but instead, trying to slow down the corrosion process of the hooks. If the eel skin lure is left in a freezer for a long time, the hook will rust and discolor the skin. Don't be alarmed. This has no effect on its fish catching ability.

They might be underused but eel skin lures fool many big stripers every year.

Another wonderful attribute of these lures is that by adding a skin to the plug we elongate the size of the lure. It is thought that big stripers prefer to feed less often than their smaller siblings, but on bigger meals. This illustrates the "expending minimum amount of energy to feed" theory, which is prevalent among those who hunt exclusively for large fish. Instead of swimming a 6-inch piece of wood or plastic in front of their noses, now you are presenting a much bigger meal and consequently a bigger profile. On some lures this can be as much as double its original size.

All these wonderful things about eel skin plugs are great, but I think there is another reason why stripers go crazy over the lures, that is the smell of the skin. Yes, the pungent, can't get it off your hands, fishy odor of eel skin. Even lures that I have rigged years ago and have been used and re-frozen many times over the years, still feature a strong eel odor. My feeling is that this is one of the primary reasons why stripers hit it hard and do not let go.

I am sure you have read over the years about the effectiveness of using half dead eels that have already caught fish. For some reason, stripers seem to key onto an eel that has already been scraped by another fish. The fact that these eels look dead or wounded might be one of the reasons. I think the other reason is that the slime has been stripped off the eel and its body odor has actually increased by rubbing against the rough mouth of a striper. This also might be why stripers hit the eel skin lure with gusto, instead of just a tap usually associated with live eels. Of course, if you are a lure aficionado, you won't mind these jarring hits one bit.

Because of the way bass hit live eels, many anglers, including yours truly, have a hard time fishing with them for exactly this reason. I am not crazy about dealing with live, slimy snakes to begin with and the "bow to the cow" technique is an acquired taste. When fishing eel skin lures, the hits are purposeful and solid, even more than when fishing with a regular lure. I will be the first to admit, that before I skinned and rigged my first eel skin lure, the process intimidated me. It took some time for me to get comfortable with it, but today I can probably skin and rig an eel skin plug in less then five minutes. In fact, I can do it much more quickly than it takes me to rig a dead eel. Initially I was hesitant to try eel skin plugs but I was convinced by my almost immediate success with this technique. When you are testing an unfamiliar technique and you manage to catch bigger fish, almost from the first cast in spots where you never caught a decent fish before, it goes a long way toward fostering confidence in that technique. As I used them more regularly, I found that I often out-fished my partners by a large margin. On one memorable night, I managed to slam half a dozen large fish while sharing a rock with a buddy, who used the same, exact lure without an eel skin.

Over the years, I have noticed a strange occurrence that happens only with rigged eels or eel skin plugs. On many nights, I've seen a good bite of fish on lures end abruptly when one angler switched to rigged eels or eel skin plugs. The stripers seem to develop lockjaw for plastic, wood or jigs, yet they readily take riggies or skins. In fact, I've seen a bite on live eels dramatically decrease when rigged eels are used. It has happened so often over past years that I have come to realize that this is not a freak occurrence. Unfortunately, I have no solid answers as to why this happens other than to say that I am delighted to be one of those who have learned to toss rigged eels or eel skin plugs. It could be that bass are attracted to the smell of dead eels or eel skins more than live ones or it could be that both rigged eels and eel skins display better and have more consistent action than the live eel does. It seems silly to make a statement that a dead eel or a lure with a skin features better action than a live eel. But, in some ways this is true. Live eels do their thing while retrieved. They might slither back and forth. They might spin or they might go into the rocks at the first sign of danger. Rigged eels and eel skin plugs, move in a much more predictable pattern which I believe big stripers actually prefer. It takes less effort for a large striper to attack either a riggie or an eel skin lure than it does to chase after a live one. After all, they can't tell the difference. By the time they do, you should have the hooks firmly implanted in their jaw.

WHICH LURE?

I'll admit I tend to be somewhat obsessed with eel skins lures. Very rarely do I look at any lure, without considering if an eel skin would look good on it. In order to keep this chapter focused on big fish, I will not bore you with details on any of a hundred available options you might have at your disposal. In fact, I will narrow the selection to the plug I prefer to use instead of going through all of them. As hunting for big bass is mostly a nighttime affair, some of the most productive daytime lures should not be considered candidates for fitting with an eel skin. I think we would all agree that poppers and pencil poppers make poor eel imitations when used in a traditional sense. In addition, lures that are designed to swim with their tails up, like Surfsters, are also not good choices. These types of lures generally have very little weight, making them poor casters to begin with. Adding the skin will not only shorten up your cast, but will kill most of the action these types of lures are designed to produce. Darters of all types fit in this category too. These lures need specific water, the faster the better, to produce their signature zigzag action. The proper weighting and angle of the slope on a darter's head, produces the lure action all by itself.

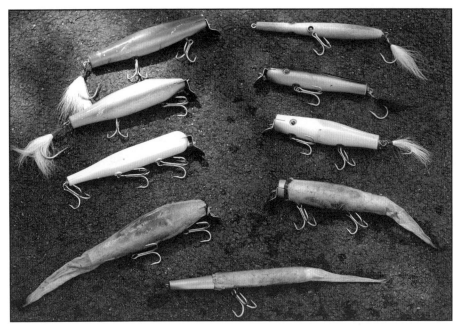

Although many lures can be fitted with eel skins, metal lip swimmers and needlefish are the best candidates.

Once you slide an eel skin over it, you're not only adding weight, but are totally throwing off the motion that the slope is made to produce. Now that we eliminated some incompatible styles of lures, we can choose the ones that would be more suited for using with eel skins and the ones that produce bigger fish.

Unfortunately, I can't help you with your final decision. Each location along the striper coast features different depths, current speeds and water movement. I would do a disservice to you, the reader, in telling you to use a particular lure and nothing else. A Cape Cod Canal surfrat, who fishes in wickedly fast currents that sometimes require jigs over 5 ounces to get close to the bottom, will have a different set of requirements than one who fishes the open beaches of Cape Cod or Long Island's South Shore. The Point Jude Eel Skin Jig for example, is very well suited for fast moving waters, like the ones found in a canal, a breachway or an inlet. An opening in the jig head allows the water to flow through the leadhead, filling the skin and giving it "body". A caster on the beaches of Cape Cod might elect to go with an eel skin draped needlefish, as he has fairly deep water in close proximity to the beach. New Jersey surfcasters have to contend with shallow, gently sloped beaches and they will probably be better served with a Danny style metal lip fitted with an eel skin than either of the two aforementioned lures. Then there are jetty jocks who patrol New York inlets, where fast and deep water can be found in close proximity to the rocks. They might elect to go with subsurface, metal lip swimmers which work very well in these waters. As you can see, each location along the striper coast presents different challenges, but opportunities too. The one common thread that ties them all together is that eel skin lures work well in any of these places.

One suggestion I can make and one I feel very strongly about, is to use large lures if you are targeting large fish. Many surfcasters hesitate to use any lure over seven inches long. The primary reason for this is that they are not willing to give up hits they might miss because of the lure size. In another words, they would rather catch a small fish than go a tide without a bump. This is absolutely the wrong way to hunt for large stripers. You bought this book because you want to increase your success in catching large stripers not because you are unwilling to get skunked. If you really want to get proficient in catching fish with lures, pick up a copy of my book "The Art of Surfcasting with Lures". Alternatively, just get really good with bucktails and you'll probably out-fish everyone around you most of the time.

There are a few reasons why I choose to use large lures in conjunction with eel skins. One of the reasons is the aggressiveness of smaller fish. These excitable little fellows will get to your lure much quicker than any large bass that might be in the area. Don't discount the fact that these large bass did not get big by chasing and attacking everything that came in sight. Using a large lure will dramatically decrease the tendency of small fish to hit it, as they generally shy away from large plugs. Adding an eel skin to a large plug and elongating its profile will drastically reduce your hit ratio because now you are presenting an even larger target to a very narrow audience: large stripers. Don't be fearful that your lure appears "too big", "too wide" or "too long." The last large fish I kept and gutted had three summer flounder, each over 17 inches, stacked in its stomach like pancakes. Considering that these summer flounder were in the early stage of decomposition, they must have been eaten within a relatively short period of time before it was caught.

Don't be fearful that your eel skin plug is too long or too big. Big stripers prefer to eat one big meal instead of many smaller ones.

Another reason for choosing a large lure, fitted with an eel skin, is the well-documented preference of large stripers to feed on large baitfish instead of many small ones. This is why you'll never see a fifty-pound brute harassing a school of spearing. They much prefer to devour a single large blackfish, eel, flounder, mackerel, bunker, herring, crab or squid. These meals provide them with a much higher caloric intake together with a much smaller loss of energy in their pursuit. Granted, eel skin plugs do not resemble any of these baits if you are looking at color or body profile. However, you are presenting a larger bait that is swinging a tantalizing tail. You may want to tell me that stripers can differentiate between blackfish and herring. OK, I'll go along with that. But let's not forget that they are primarily opportunistic feeders and will eat anything that is sizable to satisfy their hunger including their own young.

Since I believe that large stripers prefer big meals with minimal effort, it makes my choice of which lure to use simpler. In my opinion, a large metal lip swimmer fitted with an eel skin should always be in your bag if you are hunting large stripers. Danny style lures to cover the surface and calmer conditions and Atom 40 style swimmers for rougher conditions. Both of these lure styles present large targets and their slow swimming motion is very enticing to large stripers. Obviously, by using a large lure like this you will eliminate most of the small fish. There is a problem and that is finding large eel skins. You will need an extremely large eel (24 to 26 inches in length) to fit on either one of these two lures and therein lies the problem. It is very difficult to acquire extra large skins to fit these lures and you might have to search a bit to find them. If you can't find eel skins or eels large enough to fit the larger plugs, don't be discouraged. Smaller Danny and Atom 40 Junior versions are also extremely productive on big fish although the ratio of smaller fish that will be attracted to your lures will increase. These lures excel in many different types of environments, from open beaches, rocky terrains, back bays or when used around jetties. When presented with fast moving water that wraps around shallow rocky reefs, like the ones found on the north side of Montauk Point or beaches that are adjacent to inlets, go with an eel skin needlefish instead of a metal lip. Due to the shallow water generally associated with these places, you might need that extra distance these lures provide. Plus, the eel skin tail that hangs off the back of the needlefish, benefits greatly from moving water as it does not have the benefit of a metal lip to make it wiggle.

When it comes to retrieves, I like to work my needlefish as slow as possible, with small twitches every few cranks of the reel. This makes the needlefish "jump" slightly and it enhances the motion of the eel skin tail trailing behind it. Most of the hits occur on the "drop", after you twitch the lure and are picking up slack, so be diligent in trying to stay in contact with your lure. I should mention that the twitch is accomplished with a slight movement of the wrist and not by yanking the rod in a wide arc. The point is to try to make the lure appear wounded. The reason for many hits occurring after the twitch is that the lure is fluttering towards the bottom. This is almost a dead-on imitation of a baitfish that has lost its ability to swim.

With metal lip swimmers, I don't feel a need to do anything different than what I do when using metal lips without eel skins. The only different technique that I will use is limited to subsurface lures in fast water. I retrieve them with occasional sweeps of my rod. Doing this pulls the lure forward and causes them to flutter. Unlike needlefish, which are generally made to sink, the metal lip swimmer will flutter towards the top. Again, the point is to present the lure in such a way, that it resembles an injured baitfish since an injured fish does not swim in a straight line. With these lures, the hits will often occur after you resume your retrieve. I find this type of retrieve is more productive when fish are finicky and not feeding aggressively. Most of the time, I find that a straight and slow retrieve works just fine, if not even better than the sweeping one. The more important concern is to adjust the depth these metal lips are going to be swimming at. I am not going to dwell on details as I have outlined many of them in my book *"The Art of Surfcasting with Lures"* and I don't want to be repetitive. To control the depth of the lure, bend the nose wire up if you want your metal lip swimmer to go deeper. The opposite is true if you want your lure to stay on or close to the surface, bend the wire down.

WHERE TO USE THEM

Picking a location where you can use eel skin lures is as important as choosing the right lure to be fitted with an eel skin. I am a big proponent of fishing the "white water" with lures and bait. But, when using eel skin lures, the white water is more of a hindrance than an ally. I already mentioned in a previous chapter why I think that white water is not the first place I would look to hook up with a big striper. One of the reasons eel skin lures are not as effective in rough waters is the fact that rough surf is almost always associated with strong, in-your-face wind. Eel skin lures are in most cases terrible casting lures, even without an eel skin. Add an eel skin and they cast like a wet rag into the wind. Needlefish are the exception, however. If you read any of my writings over the years, you are familiar with my thinking that white water does a superb job of masking a lure and inducing a fish to hit it without a clear knowledge of what exactly it is trying to engulf. Trailing an eel skin in white water becomes almost an unnecessary addition to the lure under these conditions. The skin has a tendency to roll around in the rough water and often gets caught on the treble hooks.

When fishing the sandy beaches with eel skin lures look for calm conditions and gentle wave action, instead of white water.

The right water for targeting big stripers with an eel skin lure is often found within the confines of our inlets and breachways. Yes, the sand beaches can also be productive but still, I would look for calm to moderate conditions here, instead of the white water I usually crave. The rocky shorelines of Rhode Island, Montauk Point or many of the islands that dot the Massachusetts shore are also fantastic places to use eel skin lures. Surfcasters in New Jersey, where rocky shorelines are almost nonexistent will find most success by casting eel skin lures alongside and from atop of the many jetties that are found along the oceanfront beaches. Many small bridges were built on the back bay marshlands and serve as gateways to ocean beaches. Their bright lights attract extraordinary amounts of small baitfish during nighttime hours. This in turn draws large baitfish like herring or squid which feed on these small critters. The shadow lines that these lights create are an important feature. The striped bass will set up shop in the dark water, facing into the current and use the shadows as an ambush point. All this activity usually means that there will be some large fish prowling not just under the bridge, but along its adjoining shorelines too.

Metal lip swimmers, particularly the subsurface variety, can be absolutely deadly. You cast up current and then drift them into the shadow lines. With the strong current usually found here, a retrieve is sometimes unnecessary, you only need to keep the line tight and the metal lip should wiggle the eel skin tail under the surface. These spots are usually very productive when big baitfish like menhaden, squid or shad populate our bays in the spring. They can be even better in November, when large herring become the primary bait. There were nights when I've seen giant bass, stacked like cordwood in the bridge shadow lines, waiting for the current to deliver their meals.

Before you grab your eel skin plug and run to your favorite bridge, I have a word of caution to dispense. Since you will generally fish in close proximity to bridge abutments, you will need specialized gear. Even then, you'll probably loose as many fish as you are going to land. Considering most of your hits will come within a few feet of barnacle-encrusted abutments, you will need to keep the fish away from them. Ripping currents and cow bass will not help you in this endeavor. Most guys that specialize in this type of fishing use stiff conventional rods, 50 or 60 lb braid, with a 100-pound test leader and a locked down drag. I don't find this very appealing or sporting and you'll usually find me away from the abutments, plugging the adjoining shoreline. I find quality fish here with regularity, without having to resort to using a broomstick handle for a rod and rope for a line.

On the backside of the inlets and inlet jetties, I will often add an eel skin jig and occasionally a needlefish to my arsenal of weapons. This is another place that features fast currents and in addition, there is usually deep water within casting range. Inlets and breachways are not the only places that share these characteristics. Many ponds that drain into the ocean or the shoreline of the Cape Cod Canal feature similar water movement. Due to the increased water depth in these areas and the need to get a lure down deep fast, eel skin jigs will probably be the preferred lure with a subsurface metal lip, which moves slowly through the water, a second choice. Needlefish can be deadly, particularly during the time of slower current. Obviously, the speed of the current and depth of the water are different in each location and I cannot make a general statement without pointing this out. If you have forty feet of water where your needlefish lands, you are going to have a hell of a time getting it down deep, regardless of how slow the current is moving.

If you target boulder-strewn fields that are found in many places along the striper coast, consider yourself warned. These boulders attract many marine species and they provide food and shelter for many marine creatures. This in turn brings large stripers in the area, as they absolutely love to feast on blackfish, sea bass and scup. So hold on to your rod when fishing these spots and raise your expectation levels. In places that feature very strong currents, like the ones that wrap around Montauk Point lighthouse, a needlefish is usually my number one choice. I can cast it well up current and then just twitch it slowly as it swings down current. Oftentimes, the retrieve is only necessary to pick up the slack and stay in contact with the lure. Shallow water is often associated with these boulder fields and subsurface metal lips, although productive, can be a pain in the butt to use. You will often find, that half way through your retrieve, your lure will be buried in kelp or stuck in the rocks. This is why I chose to either wade out far enough so that I can reach deeper water with my cast or I elect to use a surface swimmer. Look for slower current and calm water conditions, as a fast moving rip will usually make your surface swimmer wiggle excessively. When I fish the rocky coves and points of Cuttyhunk, Massachusetts, I opt to go with a needlefish or a Danny style eel skin lure, because I find the current to be much slower than at Montauk. Choose your weapon carefully, according to the water conditions you have in front of you and I am certain that your big fish hook-up ratio will increase.

Sand beaches are my least favorite place to use an eel skin lure but not because they are not productive. There is some great structure within the inlets, in close proximity to my home. I have done very well in these spots over the years and I keep going back out of habit, even in years when they are not as productive. I am a big believer in fishing a limited area but fishing it hard and getting to know it well. This is why I never claimed to be an expert on any and all places along the striper coast. Any person that does is just plainly full of it. The reason he might try to sell you on his superior skills is either that he actually has something to sell you or his ego has been inflated to the size of a Goodyear blimp. I can honestly tell you that I don't spend much time tossing eel skin lures on sandy beaches.

However, I will use them on sandy beaches adjacent to inlets. As I mentioned before, I am a big believer that current enhances the action of any lure fitted with an eel skin. This is why I like to stick close to the inlet structure and benefit from its current flow. In addition, most inlets have a sandbar, which tends to curve towards the beach. This area between the sandbar and the shore acts as a funnel of sorts and the bait is channeled through it during its migration. Probing the depths of this trough with a needlefish or a surface type metal lip swimmer fitted with an eel skin can be very productive. There is usually a good number of smaller fish here, mixed in with a few quality fish. Fortunately, eel skin lures do a great job of discouraging small critters from taking a swipe at your plug. Of course, nothing ever stopped bluefish from taking a shot at any lure. However, bluefish will leave it alone after they take a bite of the tail and realize there is no meat on it. Which is a beautiful thing in my book!

USE A LURE WITH GOOD "MOJO"

There is one important part I haven't touched upon and that is confidence. After a few nights of watching me hammer fish on a local jetty using eel skin plugs, one of my friends relented and rigged one of his lures with a skin. The next night we fished side by side with similar lures both fitted with eel skins. The difference was, he wasn't catching any fish on his. After about an hour of this, I thought his plug required an inspection. Maybe his rigging process was flawed, or his hooks were the wrong size. After looking the plug over, I was surprised that I couldn't find a single thing wrong with it. The plug was fitted with an eel skin perfectly and the nose wire was bent upwards to get the lure deep into the water column. The hooks were the proper size and extremely sharp. I handed the lure back to him and said, "I can't find anything wrong with this lure. How does it produce without an eel skin on it?" His reply almost made me slip off the rock I was standing on. "What do you mean how does it work without a skin? It sucks. Never caught a fish on it even when they were blitzing. Why do you ask?" After I heard this I walked away without uttering another word. Although he is a close and trusted friend, he deserved to spend a night in frustration. He thought he was going to take a lousy plug, one that never produced for him in the past, fit it with an eel skin and it would become a deadly weapon. Wrong!!! A lure that is lousy

It is imperative to use a lure with good "mojo" in conjunction with an eel skin. A bad lure with an added eel skin is still a bad lure, only uglier.

without an eel skin will still be lousy after an eel skin has been added. Only uglier! Take that into consideration when you are picking your lure. Use your "mojo" plug for rigging, not some castaway you found in a dark corner of your garage.

You are hunting for big fish. These fish will be in the area for a limited period of time. You will have a limited time and opportunity to present your lure to them and entice them to strike. Give yourself the best possible chance and use your best stuff. Either that, or prepare yourself for a lifetime of watching the surfcaster next to you sliding monsters up onto sand. Hey, he might ask you to gaff one for him one day which will be as close as you will get to that fish of your dreams. Look, I am not suggesting that miracles will not happen. Guys with K-Mart rods and cheap line catch fish in broad daylight every day. But that's luck and I am a believer that each person makes his own luck through his or her actions. Can I make big fish come to an area I am fishing in? No. But I can find a place where they prefer to gather. I can find a tide period during which they like to feed. I can find a baitfish they like to feed on which will tell me the depth at which they will be feeding. After doing all this scouting work, I am not going to throw at them a crappy plug I have no confidence in, just because I draped an eel skin over it. You have to believe in your ability and your lure without the skin. Only then will adding an eel skin to the lure make it a deadly weapon.

RIGGING A LURE WITH AN EEL SKIN

Step One: Freeze eels until dead and then defrost them in a bucket of water. Sprinkle some Kosher salt on a paper towel and roll the eel in it. Take another paper towel and remove all the eel slime by gripping the eel tightly with paper towels and pulling towards the tail.

Step Two: Prepare the brine by mixing an equal amount of hot water and Kosher salt. Let the brine cool down completely and keep adding Kosher salt to the water until it stops dissolving. Pour the mixture into a plastic or glass container with a screw top. The container should be large enough to hold all the skins you are processing at the time.

Step Three: With a razor blade, make an incision around the body of an eel, approximately ½ inch below the gills. Just cut deep enough to cut through the skin. Nail the eel through its head to a tree, or fence post. With two pairs of pliers, one on each side of the eel, start to peel the skin by pulling downwards. Pay close attention that meat is not attached to the skin, as it starts peeling away from the body. If it is, use the razor blade to detach it from the skin. Once the skin is peeling freely, remove it in one pull downwards. The skin will now be inside-out and will have a light blue color. Cut the skin above the anal vent and discard it. Place the skin in the brine to toughen it up for a minimum of two days or for indefinite storage. Place the brine in the freezer.

Step Four: Remove all the hooks from the lure you intend to rig. Place an eel skin at the tail end of the lure and slide it towards the head, making sure that the darker side is on the top and lighter side is on the bottom of the lure. Keep pulling the skin over the lure, until there is a three-inch length of tail hanging behind the lure. This is the length I use on metal lip swimmers, because they generally have two pair of trebles. On needlefish, which usually feature one treble, I might go with a slightly longer skin. I generally use an inside-out skin that is light blue in color. It seems strange to skin an eel and then use the skin in such a way that does not reflect the color of the real thing. I find that I do better with an inverted eel skin lure, than with those rigged with the natural dark surface on the outside. As I mentioned before, this might have something to do with the fact that an inverted eel skin has a much stronger odor than a lure rigged in natural color or maybe it's just my imagination! In any event, it works for me. Feel free to experiment and come to your own conclusions.

Step Five: Adjust the skin so that its "seam" runs along the bottom of the lure and right over the swivel. With a razor blade, make a tiny incision perpendicular to the seam, right over the swivel. If you make your incision parallel to the seam, you skin might slit along the seam. Now work your swivel through the tiny incision.

Step Six: With rigging floss, fasten the skin to the lure by using a ring already grooved into the lure or by tying around the metal lip. I have not seen big difference by using one approach over another. The groove around the lure body is more convenient, but not necessary. Tie a square knot, then turn the lure over and repeat the process, finishing it with a square knot again. Now turn it to the other side and repeat the same procedure one more time. Cut the waxy floss close to the knot and dab a drop of "Zap A Gap" or similar glue on the knot. With the razor blade, cut the skin about half an inch ahead of the rigging floss and fold it back over the floss and knots.

Step Seven: Attach sharpened hooks. I prefer cut VMC Permasteel hooks which I cut and open myself using two pair of pliers. I am not a big fan of split rings, especially when it comes to adding them to my eel skin lures. Sometimes, the added length the split rings provide will cause the trebles to catch each other on every cast, making the lure useless.

I have never had a cut VMC hook open on me and I think 4X is a sufficient strength. The new, VMC 6X strong hooks are in my opinion very heavy and tend to have a negative influence on the way a lure is swimming, particularly metal lip swimmers.

Step Eight: Rinse the plug and the hooks in fresh water after each trip to the beach to get the salt off. Store the plug in the freezer in a heavy duty zip-lock freezer bag. It will be ready for you the next time you head for the beach.

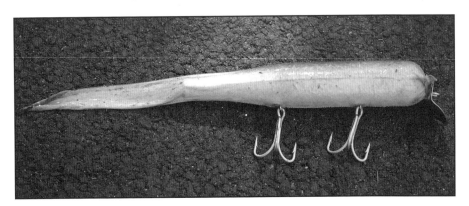

CHAPTER ELEVEN

BAIT FISHING

By "Crazy" Alberto Knie

There is a group of fishermen who cringe whenever they hear the word "chunking" because they think it is the dark side of surf fishing. However, this is a productive method which one cannot ignore when seeking quality bass on a consistent basis. Sad to say, chunking is often belittled by plug casters and flyrodders because it appears to be primitive and lacking skills or not meeting their "sporting" standards. On the contrary, those who advocate these sentiments need to jump down from their high horses and be open-minded. There are many challenges in chunking and sage bait slingers will go a great distance to perfect this technique. In other words, there is more to it than meets the eye!

Mind you, I am an opportunistic fisherman and an avid lure caster. During my forty plus years of passionate fishing, I've learned a great deal about fishing techniques. I know when to toss lures and when to chunk. Like anything else in life, there is a time and place for everything and chunking is a method that produces big stripers.

Now that I've gotten that out of the way, let's dig in deeper and find out what chunking is really all about. In order to be a good bait fisherman, there are many challenging obstacles to overcome. First of all, we are dealing with a method that will involve tapping into limited fish staging structures from the beach, rocks or other shore features. Understanding different tide stages and how tide relates to the shoreline plays a critical role in chunking, and often takes many years to master. Other critical factors are understanding bait migration, how to select the proper tackle and how to use it. Correct casting technique also plays a vital role in achieving success. Finally you have to understand the entire "patience" game. All in all, a proficient chunker is a stealthy and calculating fisherman who knows to strike when the iron is hot. It is the "six pack" fisherman, his three day old smelly bunker and his sand-spiked spinning outfit fishing under the blazing sun that gives the chunker a bad name.

PROPER TACKLE

Since this chapter is about chunking for large striped bass, a savvy bait slinger will need a rod stout enough to toss heavy payloads and strong enough to control a powerful fish. Please note that it is all about hunting for a "trophy" bass! Your tackle should be able to manage the environment (rocks, strong currents, distant sand bars, etc.) where large bass are found. The rod and reel combination needs to be well chosen to subdue large, tough fish. Any compromise on the tackle that I am about to recommend could potentially give the fish an edge and you could very well be the next person at the party weeping about how the big one got away.

We live in a high tech fishing era in which we now use rods manufactured of space age fibers that have unparalleled strength together with incredible lightness and sensitivity! Without a doubt, we are living in a very exciting high tech world. Given that, there are a variety of rod and reel manufacturers from which to choose. My favorite is the conventional Lamiglas XS12MHC rod (12' Medium Heavy Conventional). This rod is rated to cast from 6 to 16 ounces and is rated for line from 15 lbs to 50 lbs test monofilament. This 12' conventional rod allows you to cast a greater distance and it also has the power to subdue any bass that swims our oceanic waters. I've also graduated from mono to braided line as it allows me to feel the slightest pick up.

Braided line provides extra sensitivity and greater casting distance than mono. Although the rod is rated for up to 50 lb. test, it has become common practice among experienced surf fishermen to use heavier line. I spool 80 lb braid on my reels and it suits me just fine. However, extreme caution must be taken as there are many do's & don'ts when utilizing such heavy line on this rod. Please note! When snagged, do NOT try to break the line by bending the rod and pulling against the snag. You run the risk of breaking your rod! What you should do is to apply pressure on the reel's spool and walk backwards while pointing the rod in the direction of the snag. With constant pressure, the line will snap at the weakest link. Please remember that braided line does not give (zero stretch properties) therefore it will require great strength to break the braid. The most common mistake is to try to break the line by yanking the rod up & down. That will frequently break the rod and cancel the rod manufacturer's warranty policies. Most manufacturers will not honor such abuse! Another

Give yourself the best chance of landing a large fish by using proper tackle.

mistake when snagged with braided line is to cut the braid at the reel with a knife or scissors. This is not recommended. Cutting the line, and allowing it to flow loosely to sea will hurt the environment as well as causing potential harm to wading fishermen and waterfowl. So be sensitive about using braid, and be extra conscious about how you discard your fishing line.

In regard to reels, revolving spool conventional reels have much more strength than most spinners. Conventional equipment can cast a great distance. They are a good choice when targeting heavy surf caught fish. I have used many brands and I've even tricked out several reels to maximize distance and strength. My favorite reels are all without level winds. I don't need a level wind since long ago I educated my thumb to lay the line on the reel perfectly every time, thus making backlashes less likely. There are many premium reel brands, but my reel of choice is the Daiwa Saltiga Surf, which has a centrifugal spool anti-backlash brake and a fast gear ratio (5.4:1) which pulls in over 35 inches of line with every crank. It is extremely smooth and has 7 ball bearings, including anti-corrosion bearings. This reel is designed specifically with the surfcaster in mind and it has helped me land several trophy bass with great ease. With the above rod and reel combination, it is important to practice casting to prevent backlashes. Practice makes perfect, and eventually you will develop an educated thumb that will make you a proficient cow hunter.

THE CONVENTIONAL RIG

Many people use small hooks and light lines when chunking but to fish properly, it is essential to use the biggest hooks and the strongest leader possible. Contemporary hooks are manufactured from high carbon steel, the points are extremely sharp and they are covered with a corrosion resistant surface coating. This allows easy hook setting penetration together with great strength. I favor the #10 wide gap style (Octopus) and snell it with a short 10" – 15" heavy 100 lb monofilament leader into a heavy duty 150 lb swivel. This can be easily tied with an improved clinch knot. The improved clinch knot is one of the most widely used knots for tying a line to a hook, lure or swivel. Be sure to turn five turns otherwise you sacrifice knot strength. Exceeding five turns it becomes increasingly difficult to tighten properly. I use a shock leader on the end of my braided line. I slip a fish finder rig with a bead on the shock leader. Then I tie the end of the shock leader to the swivel. The bead will act like a shock absorber and prevent the fish finder from banging into the knot.

My shock leader (long leader) is 60 lb or 80 lb test and it is approximately 17' long. I use a pendulum cast by dragging the chunk from the sand (to obtain resistance for better distance casting) and I use the full 17' of shock. Why 17' you might ask? The rod is 12' long and I allow two complete turns of the shock leader onto the reel. A heavy shock leader should always be used as it helps offset fraying from the rocks and any bottom obstructions. The heavy leader also gives something substantial to grip when pulling a hooked fish from the suds. Since I tie my shock leader directly to my running braid line, it is important that the knot connecting the shock leader to the braid be tied properly otherwise that's where your weakest link lies.

In order to keep your bait in one place and prevent the waves and current from pushing your offering to shore, a pyramid sinker weighing anywhere from 6 to 10 ounces is preferred. Understanding tides and the moon phases will also help you determine the proper weight to use. Should you experience a strong current, it is wise to go heavier and keep your bait as still as possible. There are also exceptions to the rule when bank sinkers must be utilized over certain rocky, or mussel bottom areas so that they do not snag. There is an art to this madness but the key is to know your surroundings.

You may wonder whether I use fluorocarbon leader or not. I don't feel it is necessary when the water is dirty or cloudy. During bright daylight and gin clear waters, the use of fluorocarbon leader is well recommended. The added advantage of those invisible lines is that they are also abrasion resistant and are a lot stronger than regular monofilament leaders! When in doubt – simply use it!

There are many brands of braid to choose from and my experience tells me the more "weaving" strands, the rounder the braid is and the better the line will sit around the spool! The round line will provide greater casting distance and the roundness in the line will also fit the spool better than flat braids. Flat braid lines have a tendency to dig deep into the spool when fighting a large fish. If this happens you will run the risk of the line digging deeply into the spool and this will probably cost you the fish. I like the Suffix and Daiwa braids.

THE ALBERTO KNOT AND BRAIDED LINES

Years ago when braid first hit the scene, I was fortunate enough to be one of the first to use braided line. At the time it was said that it would change the way we fish. With its low diameter strength, zero stretch, extra sensitivity, flexibility, line noise reduction, faster sink rate, less current resistance and impressive casting capabilities, it truly has changed the way we fish today!

Within a short period of time, almost everyone was using braid but there was a common problem. Anglers were unsure of which knot to use to connect mono and braid. Manufacturers suggested that we tie direct or use barrel swivels. Those recommendations were not acceptable. It was during those critical days that I came up with "Alberto's Knot". This knot is the result of many sleepless hours and was inspired by the ingenuity of the Chinese Finger Trap.

The design of this knot is simple. It is intertwined and the harder you pull, the tighter the knot gets! Although it seems difficult to tie at first, it gets easier to do with practice. Like everything else in this world, the more you practice the better it will be. Originally I kept it to myself. I began showing it to several hardcore fishermen and boat captains both here in the States and in areas I have had the good fortune to fish around the world. Now it has become internationally popular wherever braid line to mono is used and I am extremely happy to share it.

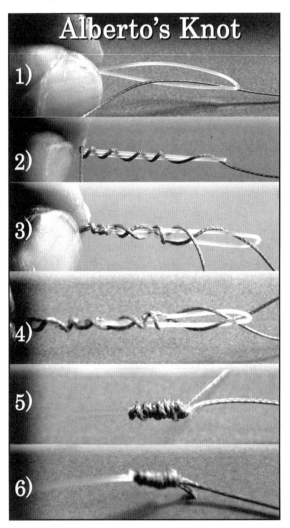

the States and in areas I have had the good fortune to fish around the world. Now it has become internationally popular wherever braid line to mono is used and I am extremely happy to share it.

When properly tied, Alberto's knot will allow the knot connection to go through the guides smoothly! When the knot is properly tied it is tested at 98% which is higher than any other knot recommended by manufacturers. Most importantly, with the use of the Alberto's knot, you will never need to use a barrel swivel again. In the long run, your rod tip will thank you for that.

Finally it is critical to remember before installing braid on a reel, you will need monofilament backing. Failure to put layers of mono on the spool will result in the braided line spinning around the spool.

THE FRESHEST BAIT

A good bait fisherman knows the importance of having the freshest bait available and he will go to great measures to obtain it. This is without a doubt the truth and one can not express enough the importance of having the freshest bait available! In the event you are not able to net or snag your own, it is critical that you have reliable sources of fresh bait. You should keep in frequent contact with your local bait shop or perhaps you can tip the staff a little extra to reserve the freshest bait for you. I don't care how you keep in good graces with the shop but it needs to be done!

When you are trying to master the chunking methodology, obtaining the freshest bait is just the very beginning of the process. Transporting the freshest bait to the fishing grounds is the next challenge. In truth, savvy fishermen always take great pride in their baits and here are some of the tips you need to know. Fresh bait has slime and the slime is one of the key factors why fish are so attracted to it. After casting your offering, the slime spreads similar to a chum slick, and it will pull fish from great distances. Given that, the importance of preserving freshness is critical and that can be done by zip locking the fresh bait and preventing the ice water from touching the bait. Please note that freshwater or ice cubes can contaminate the slime and that is a big problem. Fresh bait can also be kept for only a day or two! Every day it sits in your refrigerator, it will become softer and it will not stay on the hook very long.

RIGGING WITH BAITS

Certain fish parts also play a role when targeting large stripers. You will often see folks fighting over the head of the bunker. Why fight for the head part you might ask? The reason is simple. The head part has many positive fish attracting attributes. The bunker's eye catches the attention of the bass, the gills retain a good amount of juice and the head will stay on the hook for a longer period of time than a simple chunk. The proper hook placement should be just above the gills ensuring the end of the hook's barb will be exposed. Be sure to inspect the hook's point for it is common to have a loose scale embedded into the point. Ignoring the loose scale will prevent the hook from penetrating the striper's jaw. The proper head rigging method (setting the hook above the gills) will guarantee a positive hook set when engulfed by a large bass.

The second most important bait part is the neck and guts. Many people often discard the guts and that is a monumental mistake. A fresh gut also makes a great mini chum slick. Simply grab the guts and hold the fish's heart – be sure to penetrate the heart and keep the guts intact when hooking the rest of the chunk. Unquestionably, the guts and neck parts are my second choice and I have caught countless bragging size bass.

The remaining bunker pieces and the tail portion are my least favorite parts but when distance casting is vital, I will use them. Otherwise I give these to a friend and watch him catch the trash fish (dogfish, skates, etc) that share the same bass grounds.

In order to retain its flavor, slime and texture, place the bait in a Ziploc bag and ice it immediately, making sure that it does not come in direct contact with ice.

THE BITE EXPECTATIONS

Before I get involved in this topic, it is very important not to dead stick with a sand spike! Although dead sticking is commonly used, I find it difficult to detect the slightest tap from a finicky bass and it often results in lost opportunities. I will confess that I've had many soft pick-ups only to realize it was an impressive fish on the end of the line. I've also noticed that big fish can detect the most unnatural resistance and they will quickly drop the offering, never to give an angler a second chance.

The saying that bass don't get big for being stupid is true! The biggest are the slickest and will pass on an awkward presentation. Seasoned anglers will hold on to the rod and feel for subtleties and feed line back to the fish to allow ample time for the fish to commit. The slightest indication can be felt only by holding the rod and by having the reel in free spool. What do you do if the right fish comes along? With a soft pick-up, simply take two steps forward and allow the running line to belly. Pay close attention because a wary fish will just nudge the bait especially when she is not hungry. Allow the fish to take its time and as soon as she picks up the offering, give line and let the fish-finder rig do its job. The fish will slowly take the bait for a short ride. By feeding line to the fish, the bass should decide it's an easy meal and engulf the bait. Only then she will start to move and you need to lower the rod by pointing it toward her. When the line is taut, that's when you need to cross her eyes with all you've got! This cat & mouse play is common during calm water conditions and it is usually not detected by dead sticking.

WHEN THE BITE GETS TOUGH...

There have been times when the bite was tough but I always managed to catch a few bass. One time I announced the bite play by play and the talk went like this. The night was young but the tide was forming beautifully. The calm wind was a sign of a slow night but I knew there were big fish in the area because there was plenty of bait movement and we would hear an occasional distant explosion. I could envision bass massacring baitfish by the edge of a skinny water drop-off. It was just a waiting game and we waited patiently. I knew the fish would pass near us. We positioned ourselves in between a pronounced bass highway path and continued to wait.

It wasn't long when my line started to move from my free-spooled reel. It moved so slightly but I knew there was a finicky fish examining my bait. I whispered to my friend, "She is smelling my bait now." My partner gave me a look of disbelief. Then I said, "Hold it, she dropped it. Darn! Oh, oh wait, she just swam around my line." Again, my friend was thinking that I was just joking around. I held my breath and now I whispered softly, "She is back and now she is sniffing my bait again." I fed her some more line and dropped my rod down slightly to allow her to take my offering. "Oh... yeah, she's got it in her mouth and she is now swimming around with the bait in her mouth." My friend saw my line going out and I continued to feed her more line. She didn't sense any restriction and she was now ready to engulf it. I put my reel in gear while my rod was pointed at 11'o clock and allowed her to bow the rod pointing toward her. I set the hook with great authority and the fight was on! She immediately peeled off line against my drag. When she finished taking me for a ride, I started to pump her back slowly and my partner was completely in awe. She peeled off more line but I knew she had no chance because she was already out of her domain and along the flat part of the ocean's crest. I managed to lip her. She was a respectable mid 30 pounder. We took a quick shot with the camera and she swam away to fight another day.

During rough water conditions, fish can be careless but during the calmest nights, that's when you really need to be stealthy and sharp. Also take note that fresh bait can be dunked for no longer than 10 minutes or so. By constantly changing the fresh bait, you will generate a large chum slick and if there are any fish in the vicinity, they will respond immediately. If that does not happen move to another spot or hole and waste no time on that tide.

LOCATING THE PRODUCTIVE AND NOT-SO PRODUCTIVE STRUCTURE

Locating prime water in the surf requires more thought than meets the eye. You not only have to cast your bait out into the surf but it must be kept in the strategic feeding zone while waves try everything possible to wash your bait back to shore. These are just some of the obstacles you will face but that's just part of this challenging game. The biggest challenge is identifying productive waters. This is easily done by a seasoned angler, but if you are just learning the ropes, it can be rather difficult. The beginner is often not sure what to look for. The best times to find new uncharted grounds are to spend some time during the day when the tide is low, and seek the obvious deep pockets along an inlet or point.

Locating a "soft structure" is extremely rewarding and it can be done only by low tide daytime scouting trip. At times finding a secluded outer bar is all it takes and it could be your best shot to catch your personal best.

Here are the reasons why a soft structure is so good. Predators such as large bass frequenting the surf are programmed when current and waves create churning conditions and disorient any baitfish and make it easier to ambush them.

It is also apparent that the mouths of inlets and rivers are perfect spots and such areas should never go unchecked. The downside to such areas is that they are often crowded. A lot of commotion will cause the biggest and finickiest fish to shy away. On the other hand, if you concentrate on the same spot during the late wee hours of the night with little human distractions, your catch ratio will

Locating "soft structure" is extremely rewarding and the best time to do it is during low tide in the daytime.

increase dramatically. In other words, it is good to constantly look for new spots, but when you are unsuccessful, fish the common spots during the "non human" hours and there is a good chance that you will catch a cow bass.

SEASONS AND TIDES

Unquestionably there is always a right place and time for productive bass fishing but it is all relative to knowing their whereabouts. If you are a scholar and have done your homework, you will realize that the striper migration is a cycle and they will be at certain locations during the spring and they will be back during the fall. The only way to confirm their whereabouts is by putting in time on the water and paying close attention to the local tides and bait migration. There is no substitute for this and it is the best way to see first hand what is happening on your favorite grounds. With that said, it is safe to say that in our local striper waters, the bass will migrate from their Chesapeake and Hudson River wintering grounds along the coast up to northern Massachusetts waters. Intercepting them can be challenging at times but following these simple rules will guide you to their whereabouts. During the month of May and throughout most of June, the stripers are scattering north along our coast. The same goes for September and well into November. They are returning south and your probable odds of intercepting them are high during these months!

Wind direction has a big impact on your local waters and understanding how it affects your local water is critical. Wind can dirty your area and it also moves your baitfish around. Given such parameters, weather forecasts are important in determining where you focus your efforts. After a while you will understand what areas are best on different winds and whether they are fishable or weedy. Ultimately you have to learn your area by putting in the time.

In regard to tides, in my mind tide plays a critical role when chasing trophy fish! My favorite tides are the few hours around the slack period. This may come as a surprise but you can ask any seasoned cow hunters and they will concur. The majority of my prime spots are best within the hour before or after the high or low slack phases. If you are in doubt, simply glance at the shape of a large fish and the broom like tail with a heavy silhouette. Her shape will reveal that she is a lazy opportunistic feeder. She will rest during most of the strong current and reserve her energy while she waits for the water to slow down. Then she will feed relentlessly during that short slack phase. That is why it is of monumental importance to know your area well and wait for that epic feeding phase around any given structure.

THE MIND SET AND PLANNING THE GAME

Just because you have read this chapter doesn't necessarily mean that you are ready to go. All the information provided in this chapter will not do you any justice unless you actually walk the beach and start putting these ideas to use. After all, it is up to each individual to absorb the invaluable learning experiences that being on the water has to offer. Then you will realize what needs to be done in order to be a successful chunker. This will give you the foundation to find and hook that elusive fish of your dreams. The preparation before the hunt sets a tone and course for that fishing trip. Therefore it is essential to plan your strategy and fish the plan accordingly. Once you've taken these fundamentals to heart, I am confident that you will have a good grasp on the areas you like to fish and the fish you are likely to target. Most important, you will understand the art of tracking the elusive cow at any given time of the season.

Furthermore, as an added incentive to your chunking exploration, I am disclosing a few rules that will help you locate your dream fish. These added tips are often overlooked but should play a critical role in your everyday chunking success.

THE BENEFITS OF LOGGING

Be sure to log your trips and chart your tides, moon, wind, locations and everything else that you might think will help you in the long run. In this process, you will soon discover distinctive patterns that no one else will know. You need to pay close attention to the details recorded in your log because your unique findings will help you to be in the game and zone. Overall, it pays to log as much information as possible and it should be treated as your personal diary. Review your log frequently and see if you can establish relationships between successful trips and the elements (tide, moon, wind, etc.) that you have recorded. I cannot stress enough the importance of logging!

TAKE A HIKE

In today's world, everything is about convenience. I can't tell you how many times I've seen folks fishing in close proximity to their vehicle or fishing the "human" hours. You can call it laziness or convenience, but truth be told, many prime spots are overlooked because folks won't make the walk. With today's surf fishing popularity, it pays dividends to walk and fish secluded areas where few will venture. It also pays to sacrifice your time and fish the late hours of the night. My motto is simple. I fish when the majority of fishermen are sleeping and dreaming of fish, while I am on the water catching their dreams.

KEEPING IT STEALTHY AND HUSHED

Those who put in their time and work hard for their fish are usually rewarded for their efforts. They also catch many fish consistently because they make a point of keeping it "hush." In reality, no one needs to know until the bite is over. I am not trying to say that I am selfish but in all the years that I've been fishing the suds, I've learned to keep it quiet and tell only those you trust. Call this old school or anything you like, but it is important to keep it quiet because you really don't want anyone else jumping in your parade uninvited. Keeping your bite secret is always a good thing and it is a validation and reward for your hard work. I also make sure not to leave any trace of my activities along the beach. I believe this is good practice because it allows everyone to make an honest effort to learn on their own. By giving the spot and specific time you take a most valuable lesson away from them. This sport is about the hunt and the "How To", never the spot!

Respecting the resource will go a long way toward insuring that the next generation of surfcasters will enjoy this wonderful fishery.

FISHING THE STORM MYTH

I am sure that at some point in time you heard about fishing during big storms or a heavy blow. That holds true to an extent but let's be smart about it because it can be a life-threatening proposition. First of all allow me to clarify this phenomenon. Fish are like any wild animal and they possess extra survival sagacity. Fish can sense the cold fronts and they certainly sense the rapid sudden change of the weather. Under those conditions, they put on the feed bag because they are uncertain when their next meal will be. You have to know when to fish it and when to run for cover. The best time to fish it is a few hours before the developing storm and the first few hours while the water is still clean. Once the water clarity or visibility drops that's the time to run for cover. I've fished the worst conditions with great success only to be chased away by law enforcement. The truth of the matter is that you should fish smart and always remember that no fish is worth dying for.

RESPECTING THE FISH AND THE FUTURE

Always respect the resource. This is one of the most neglected aspects of fishing and it needs to be addressed. Whether you are in it for the fun and excitement or for the meat, be sensitive about the fish. Back in the early days prior to the striped bass moratorium of the 1980's, who would have thought that we could have depleted an entire biomass? Sad to say we did! Thanks to environmental groups and the Department of Conservation, the striped bass population rebounded. However, with today's fishing popularity, it is important to preserve what we have now. We all have to make sure that history doesn't repeat itself. While the art of chunking is a very productive method for catching many trophy fish, it is important to preserve our stock. We need to make sure to have bass for many generations to come. While the law allows us to take a few, we need to practice catch and release. This will assure that we can continue to catch these magnificent fish that we so adore for many years to come. On this final note, enjoy the chunking aspect of this sport and catch'em up!

CHAPTER TWELVE

BUCKTAILS

By John Skinner

My pulse quickened as I felt a series of bottom taps as my sparsely tied 4-ounce bucktail swept downcurrent of my position on the west jetty of Moriches Inlet. It was the first time in the thirty minutes I had been fishing that I finally felt like I had hit the correct combination of location, jig weight, and presentation to put my bucktail in the strike zone. It normally didn't take so long to get things right, but a recent Nor'easter had altered the bottom structure, and the night was so dark that I couldn't read the rip visually and had to feel my way around. I chuckled at the thought that I had actually gotten excited over an encouraging frequency of bottom bumps. After many fruitless casts, my sudden feeling of anticipation was interrupted by a sharp tap that was easily distinguishable from the collisions of my jig with the bottom structure. I set the hook hard, and held the fish in place just long enough to back down slightly on the nearly locked drag. With the help of the current, the fish set a course for East Moriches. With no obstructions, boats, or other interference to worry about, I enjoyed the run and spent the next ten minutes working to regain the line. The fish was whipped by the time I pulled it to the base of the jetty. With the help of my head lantern, the fish was lip-gaffed easily. It wouldn't qualify as a trophy by most standards, but the 38-pounder was a damn good fish that certainly made my night. Although it was the only one that broke 25 pounds that night, several more quality fish fell to that jig before a change in current speed altered the bite.

INLET BUCKTAILING

Bucktailing the ocean inlets of the Northeast is one of the most productive means of catching 30- to 40-pound plus bass on artificials. Anglers who score quality fish with consistency with this method tend to focus their efforts on one or two specific inlets. All of my inlet fishing is done in Moriches and Shinnecock Inlets on Long Island's eastern South Shore. Big bass can be counted on to be in these inlets from early May through early December, and bucktails are unmatched in their ability to work effectively through the bulk of the tide cycle when the currents are strong. As I wrote about in this book's live eeling chapter, we can count on stripers hugging the inlet bottom as they use the irregular bottom structure to break the current.

I have a simple objective when bucktailing inlets – glide the jig near the bottom. If you can accomplish this, you'll connect with quality bass. Unfortunately, doing it right exists in a narrow window that sits somewhere between dragging your jig ineffectively through the sand, and having your jig ride too high in the water column as it's blown downcurrent by the force of the moving water. Where you cast, how long you let the jig sink, how fast you retrieve, and the weight of your bucktail are the major variables that determine whether you meet the objective.

THE JIGS

When inlet fishing, I carry as many as eight different weight bucktails that range from 1.5 to 6 ounces. The 1.5-ounce is used very near slack water. The 6-ounce jigs are used only in fast deep water. If you're fishing the west jetty of Moriches near a Full or New Moon, these are sometimes the only bucktails that will stay in the strike zone in the middle of the tide. The 6-ounce jigs are very tiring to cast and retrieve against the current, so I use them only as a last resort when the fish are hitting and nothing else will get down to them. Most of my inlet bucktailing is done with jigs in the 2- to 4-ounce range. I use a Smiling Bill style jighead, but for no reason other than they're the most common and I have molds for that jig style for everything between 1/8 and 6 ounces.

I generally carry only two colors for inlet bucktailing; white and wine red. I never feel that white is the wrong color, but there are nights when I feel I have an advantage using wine red. Yellow and chartreuse are two other popular colors that work very well. I limit myself to two colors for practical reasons. If I'm carrying six different weight bucktails in two colors and have a spare of each, I'm already up to 24 jigs. My jigs are tipped with a 6-inch strip of red Uncle Josh pork rind. I prefer #56 rind, but the easier to find #70 works just fine. The 7-inch #57 strips also work well. The red strips are red on top and white on the bottom. The white side should be fished down, because this matches the typical fish-coloring scheme of light on the bottom and darker on top. Some anglers do well tipping their jigs with soft plastic curly grub tails in the 6-inch range. Minor details such as whether to fish a grub tail or a 7- or 6-inch pork strip are not nearly as important as becoming comfortable with what you choose and knowing how to apply it.

There are minor details that can make or break your

Changing current conditions require adjusting the weight of the bucktails you are using in order to keep the lure in the strike zone.

trip – or season. One of the most important is the hook sharpness of the jigs you're throwing. I check the sharpness of every jig hook before each trip and use a hook file to touch up any hook that's not razor sharp. As I mentioned in the eeling chapter, the larger fish have very tough mouths. Due to the belly in the line that's induced by the inlet current, drilling a hook home is made difficult. On nights with a crosswind, it can become downright frustrating. I keep a sharpening stone with me while I'm fishing to touch up any hooks that dull by being banged against the jetty rocks.

After repeated filings, the point of the jig hook will shorten and become stubby. While you may still be able to file what feels like a sharp point on this, it's not worth risking a good fish. I learned early on that those stubby hooks result in lost fish no matter how sharp they feel to the touch. When I think the hook point has shortened too much due to repeated filings, the jig head gets melted down.

RETRIEVES AND TARGETS

I use two different retrieve styles when bucktailing inlets. The first involves a slow retrieve. If I have water moving from my left to right, I'll cast to about the 11 o'clock position, let the jig settle a bit, and then start a slow and steady retrieve. Most of the hits with this approach will come when the jig is barely past the 12 o'clock position. When the jig sweeps past the 1 o'clock position, the force of the current will push the jig higher in the water column and out of the strike zone. At that point I'll burn the jig back and make another cast. The slow retrieve approach will work only if the water isn't very deep or moving too fast. Only experience with a particular piece of water will tell you whether or not this is the correct presentation. In general, I've found this approach to work best with jigs in the 1.5- to 2.5-ounce range.

If I don't feel that I'm staying in the strike zone on a slow retrieve, then I'll use what is probably the more common method that you'll see used from the inlet jetties. With the water moving from my left to right, I'll cast to the 11 o'clock position, let the jig settle a few seconds, take a crank or two to make contact with the jig, and then just hold on with my rod at a convenient striking angle as I let the jig bounce downcurrent. With this approach, most of my hits come a little further downcurrent than when I'm retrieving, and closer to the 1 o'clock position. As the jig slides further downcurrent, the push of the water will lift it out of the strike zone, and I'll usually crank it back quickly. If no one is fishing downcurrent of my position, there is another option at this point. Instead of cranking it back in, I'll hold on and let the jig sweep in closer to the jetty. As it does, it will eventually hit shallower water and once again find a near-bottom strike zone. For good or bad, it may also swing in close to submerged jetty rocks. It's bad if you snag one, but can be very good if you catch the attention of a bass using a boulder to break the current.

My approach is based purely on experience. I know how long to let the jig sink before starting my retrieve because I'm familiar with where I'm fishing. If I weren't, I'd make a few casts and let the jig sink to the bottom to determine the depth. By paying close attention to your line on the descent, you'll be able to tell when the jig hits the bottom. I've spent a lot of time bucktailing the inlets that I fish, and I'm at a point where, with a glance at the water, I have a very good idea of which jig to throw and how to retrieve it for each target that I'm focusing on. When I bucktail an inlet, I see the water in front of me as many different targets. One of the biggest mistakes I see on a jetty is when an angler guns every cast for maximum distance and keeps repeating the delivery over and over without hooking up. It's important to keep in mind that when fishing an inlet jetty, fish might be holding anywhere from the end of the cast to the base of the rocks. If you're aligned with a dropoff running perpendicular to the jetty, the sweet spot might be half a cast out. If you're downcurrent of a slight bend in the jetty, you'll probably have a rip running parallel to the rocks. The only way to work these different areas is to vary the distance on the casts. Because the water moves at different speeds depending on the distance from the jetty, you'll also need to vary the weight of your bucktail and possibly your retrieve speed.

Familiarity with currents is just as important in the inlets as it is in places like the Cape Cod Canal.

For example, to get in the strike zone at the end of a long cast I might use a 4-ounce jig and let it bounce downcurrent without retrieving. If I want to work a boil a half cast out, then a 3-ounce with a slow retrieve might suffice. It may take only a 2.5-ounce to properly fish a flip cast intended to cover the water near the base of the rocks. If I'm not catching, I'll keep making little changes in hopes that I'll start connecting. I try my best to always know where my last cast landed and how I retrieved so that if I get hit, I'll be able to repeat the delivery.

There was a time when I carried nothing but bucktails when I fished an inlet, but I now save a little space in the surf bag for large soft plastic swim shads. Although this is a bucktailing chapter, these swimbaits are worth a few words because they have their place in this style of fishing. I carry a few 7- and 9-inch bunker-pattern Tsunami swim shads on all of my inlet bucktailing trips. These do an excellent job of getting into the strike zone, and bass love them. From my experience, they work best on the slower portions of the tide. Thanks to graphite rods and braided line, it's easy to know when a swim shad is swimming properly because you can feel the tail pulsating. My approach is to let the jig fall to the bottom, take a fast crank or two, and then maintain whatever retrieve speed produces a pulsating tip. You'll be able to feel when you have it right.

For me, one of the most motivating aspects of fishing an inlet is knowing that the current speed is changing constantly. This is especially true during the period of two hours on either side of slack current. Between the changing current speed and all of the potential fish holding areas within casting range, I can stand on the same rock all night and never feel like I'm beating a dead horse. If the jetty isn't crowded and I have room to move around, I'll keep rock hopping in an area that I know has potential. This opens up a whole other dimension of possibilities. Even on the slowest nights, I fully believe there are bass in the inlet and maybe the next move, or a cast to another spot, or a change in current speed is going to pay off. That reward may be a single hit, but the chances are very good with this type of fishing that it will be from a quality fish. This optimistic mindset helps me get through the slow times and often keeps me on the rocks long enough to turn slow trips into good ones.

UNDERSTANDING CURRENT

Understanding and anticipating the current is one of the most important aspects of fishing an inlet. A tide calendar will tell you the times of high and low tides, but it will take some familiarity with the inlet you're fishing to know how that translates to when slack water occurs. High slack water is the period between incoming and outgoing current when the water stops moving before changing direction. As a specific example, the east side of Moriches Inlet experiences high slack water approximately two hours after the time listed on the tide calendar for high tide. Low slack occurs more than two hours after low tide. It can be difficult to understand how the current can be rushing in while the tide is dropping, but this occurs because the bay behind the barrier island is rather large and is being fed by a narrow inlet. Its height lags behind that of the ocean. So even though the water level of the ocean may have started to fall, the bay's height still needs time to catch up.

Most tide charts have two pieces of information associated with a high or low tide; the time it occurs, and the height above or below mean low water. For example, if the number "2.9" accompanies the time of high tide, this means that the water height at high tide will be approximately 2.9 feet above the height of an average low tide. These numbers change with the moon phase, and can be used to help anticipate current speeds.

Over time, I've learned that the current in Moriches Inlet on a 3.0 is about average, above 3.5 is screaming, and below 2.7 is relatively slow. Being able to anticipate the current speeds helps me choose where to fish and what weight bucktails to bring. Extreme weather exerts some influence over the current speeds and the times of slack water, but under normal conditions, the numbers are dependable.

INLET TACKLE

To handle a big fish in the current, you'll need an outfit with a lot of stopping power. Most of my inlet bucktailing is done with an 11-foot graphite rod based on a Lamiglas GSB1321M blank. I'll occasionally drop down to the 10-footer (GSB1201M) when I know I won't have to throw more than 4 ounces. In either case, I match the rod with a Penn 706 spooled with 50-pound-test braided line. You could get away with fishing

Strong tackle is often needed in inlets to cast heavy bucktails, deal with strong currents, and fight big fish like this one.

30-pound-test braid, but I prefer the extra margin of error provided by the 50-pound, especially with a big fish being pushed along the rocks in rough water.

At the end of the main line I use a Palomar knot to attach a 44-inch leader of 50-pound-test fluorocarbon with a barrel swivel on one end and a #54 Duolock snap on the other. Some anglers prefer to tie the jig directly to the leader, and this is certainly the safest approach. I use the snap because I change jigs frequently and I don't want to be cutting into my leader and tying a new knot with every change. Unfortunately, I pay a price for this flexibility. At least once a season, a fish will bite down on the jig head and work the snap open. When this happens, the wire straightens easily and both the jig and fish are lost. If I'm into fish and don't expect to be changing my jig anytime soon, I'll cut the snap off and tie direct.

I use a long leader to facilitate landing fish. In areas where I can safely get close enough to the water's edge, I can slide most fish less than 20 pounds up the rocks by grabbing the leader. If the fish is over 20 pounds and it's too dangerous to get to the water's edge, I'll use a gaff, even though I rarely intend to keep a bass. My gaff is an 8-footer that I built with a relatively small gaff hook. In most instances, I can easily lip gaff a fish by sticking the hook under or in its mouth. This doesn't damage the fish any more than the jig hook does, and it saves the fish from the stress of being banged around at the base of the rocks. The gaff's long handle allows me to complete the landing from a higher and safer position. In this respect, I consider the gaff a piece of safety equipment because it helps keep me out of harm's way on rough nights.

GO HOME IN ONE PIECE

Safety is a serious concern when fishing inlet jetties. Lives have been lost doing this kind of fishing. If you end up in the water in a strong current, especially on the outgoing tide, the odds of a happy ending aren't in your favor. Your first priority should be to make sure you never slip or get swept into the inlet. Always wear some sort of non-slip footwear, such as Korkers or studded wading shoes. I prefer rain pants and studded wading shoes and try to avoid wearing waders on the jetty. It goes without saying that fishing with other people around is safer than fishing alone. There was an incident on the

John Skinner puts safety high on his list. Notice a gaff, neck light and head light, all ready to assist him in landing this big fish.

Cupsogue jetty in the late 90s when, to the horror of several jetty anglers, a man slipped from the rocks and was swept into the ocean by the ebbing current. It was dusk, and there wasn't a boat in sight. One of the regulars hustled back to his truck and called 911, and the Coast Guard responded. By then it was dark. The Coast Guard skiff followed the current out, and miraculously rescued the angler. To say he was lucky is an understatement, but if someone wasn't there to make the call, it's very unlikely he could have survived. If you insist on fishing alone, consider spending $100 for a Sospenders-type inflatable PFD. You won't even know you're wearing it.

Even though most of the best inlet fishing occurs on the night tides, familiarize yourself with the rocks during the day. You should know where you'd be able to land your fish before you ever set the hook. I'll often choose where to fish based on my ability to land a fish when I hook up. Don't let the sight of a trophy bass hanging from your jig at the base of the rocks cloud your better judgment. No fish is worth your life.

RESPECT FOR OTHERS

Jetty fishing has certainly become more crowded over the last decade. Proper etiquette and consideration for fellow anglers goes a long way toward making the experience enjoyable and productive for everyone. If you're a newcomer on a jetty, know your place. Assume that the other anglers there are regulars who have invested a lot of time in their passion. If you're smart, you'll keep your distance and observe. Watching an accomplished jetty angler bang away at fish will teach you more than I ever can in these pages. If you think the fastest way to catching is getting close to the successful angler so you can cover the same water he is, you'll likely be in for an unpleasant reception and enough crossed lines for you to rethink your strategy.

Leave plenty of space between yourself and others. Fish as they do. If guys on both sides of you are gunning long casts with 3-ounce jigs, you may need to do something similar to stay in synch. When I'm in that situation and want to work water closer to the rocks, I'll watch the others and time my deliveries so that I don't interfere with what they're doing. Inlets have sweet spots, but you're often better off on your own in a slightly less productive area than you are sharing a dropoff with five other

Jetties can get very crowded, especially when the bite is on. Because of close quarters, everyone has to be using a similar technique and lures; otherwise a tangle will be inevitable.

guys. I rarely fish the best spot on the Cupsogue jetty on the outgoing tide. I know where it is and how to fish it, but it's almost always too crowded for my enjoyment. Instead, I fish a lesser spot that I almost always have to myself and I'm convinced that I do better than if I tried to deal with the fine gentlemen who seem to always be on the good ebb spot.

SHALLOW WATER BUCKTAILING

Although inlets are my favorite places for targeting large bass with bucktails, the jigs account for trophies wherever they're found. In any area with strong currents and relatively deep water, such as near bridges, much of what I've said concerning inlet fishing applies. In other settings, such as along shallow rocky shorelines and open sand beaches, a different approach is required.

Many trophy stripers have fallen to bucktails fished from rocky shorelines, such as those found on both sides of Montauk Point. My objective in this type of environment is very similar to when I'm bucktailing an inlet – swim the jig near the bottom with a slow to moderate retrieve. Note that I use the words "glide" and "swim" when I describe fishing a bucktail. For reasons I don't understand, I've often observed novice anglers attempting to bounce bucktails along the bottom. If you're fishing over a rocky bottom, this is nearly impossible without getting hung up. I

Rocky beaches can be excellent places to do some shallow water bucktailing, but they often require the use of lighter-weight bucktails.

impart very little action to my bucktails other than an occasional short lift. I do a fair amount of scuba diving, and have had the chance to watch all sorts of striper prey in their natural surroundings. I don't recall any of them hopping along the bottom. A flounder or fluke glides. A porgy or small sea bass swims. My other anti-bounce influence comes from when I used to bucktail from boats in the Fisher's Island Race and Plum Gut. The technique there is to drop the 3-way bucktail and sinker rig to the bottom, pick it up a couple of cranks, and then just hold it. You watch the fish finder and try to follow the bottom contour while gliding the jig through the rips. No extra action is imparted on the jig. This is a deadly technique used by commercial pinhookers to load their boats with bass, and has helped convince me that little more than a straight retrieve is needed for bucktails to be effective.

The objective of trying to swim the bucktail near the bottom on a slow to moderate retrieve will dictate lure and gear selection. The first thing to consider is the water depth on the end of the cast. If we use Montauk as an example, there is rarely more than 8 or 10 feet of water on the end of a bucktail cast. If we want to use a slow to moderate retrieve without snagging bottom, this will dictate that we use a jig in the ½- to 1 ½-ounce range. Under calm to moderately rough conditions, I'll probably go with a ¾- or 1-ounce. If casting distance is an issue, I'll tip the jig with a 4-inch strip of #50 Uncle Josh pork rind. This relatively small strip has little air resistance on the cast and won't cut too much into casting distance. Its

length is just enough to add an enticing flutter to the end of the jig. If the water I want to fish is close enough, I'll use a 5 ¼ - inch #70 strip because the larger profile will allow the jig to be worked on a slower retrieve without hanging in the structure. I do most of my daytime bucktailing with white jigs, but I always carry a few fluorescent green jigs because they seem to have an edge in stained water and do a good job of standing out in dense bait schools. I also carry green pork rind and often fish these strips with white jigs for a little touch of color. It's also hard to go wrong with red pork rind.

The jig's hair density is another important consideration. A sparsely tied bucktail will cast further and swim deeper than a bucktail of equal weight that has been bulked out with a lot of hair. There usually isn't very much variation in hair density among new commercially tied jigs, but it takes little more than a bluefish or two to thin out the hair.

Slower nighttime retrieves require the use of lighter weight jig heads, or bucktails with more hair. Don't fret about your casting distance; the fish will often be feeding very close to shore.

With the exception of when I'm inlet fishing, I always crush the barbs on my bucktail hooks. This allows for much easier hook penetration and better hooksets. As long as you maintain a bend in the rod, there's no risk of losing a fish because of a crushed barb. I avoid crushing the barbs when I inlet fish because it's sometimes difficult to maintain firm contact with a fish at the base of the rocks in rough conditions or when descending the rocks to land a fish. When fishing bucktails with crushed hook barbs, avoid using the pre-cut holes on the pork rind strips because the strips can slide off the hook. It's easy to make a new, smaller hole in front of the pre-cut slit by pushing firmly with the hook point of the jig.

My shallow water bucktailing technique couldn't be simpler – start and maintain a slow to moderate retrieve as soon as the jig hits the water. As long as you're not snagging bottom in this narrow water column, you'll be in the strike zone. You'll likely need to pick the retrieve speed up as you hit the shallows to avoid snagging. This shallow white water often holds fish, and bucktails do an excellent job of staying productive in the turbulence. As Zeno mentions elsewhere in this book, pay attention to the wave patterns and time your casts to work under the whitewater blankets where possible.

Bucktails work well in the shallow night surf, but a couple of adjustments need to be made. As with any night fishing, you'll need to slow down your retrieve. If you do this with the same weight jigs used on the faster daytime retrieves, you'll have trouble staying off the bottom. The bucktails I carry at night will have lighter weight heads and more hair than my daytime jigs. Fortunately, the fish are often a little tighter to the shore at night, and this will help compensate for the loss of casting distance that will be experienced with the less aerodynamic jigs

Rod choice is a matter of personal taste, but if I'm throwing lures in the 1-ounce range, I'd very much like to avoid doing that with the same 11-footer that I use for fishing the inlets. If it's not very rough or crowded, I'll try to go with my 9-foot graphite that was wrapped on a cut down Lamiglas GSB1201L blank. With one foot cut from the butt of the blank, the rod makes a superb stick for throwing small bucktails and still offers enough stopping power to put the brakes on a good fish. I match this rod with a Van Staal 200 spooled with 30-pound-test braid. If the situation calls for something more substantial, I'll fish a 10-foot rod based on a

Lamiglas GSB1201M with a Penn 706Z spooled with 30- or 50-pound-test braid.

The shallow water bucktailing discussion to this point covers fishing under calm to moderately rough conditions. If you're fishing a howling Nor'easter, complete with 30-knot-plus winds and high seas, you'll likely be best served by an 11-footer and bucktails in the 3-ounce range. Under these extreme conditions, there'll be little else you can do other than fire the jig up-sweep and do your best to stay in contact with it as you pull it through the raging surf. There are limited productive areas to fish under these conditions. These places are generally well known and require that all involved pay attention to and stay in synch with anglers on both sides.

The open sand beaches are probably the easiest to bucktail effectively, but usually don't have the big fish potential of inlets and rocky shorelines. The ease of fishing comes from the fact that the water column is narrow, but the bottom is forgiving. If your jig is too heavy, you'll feel excessive bottom dragging and you can simply make adjustments to weight, hair density, and pork rind size until you hit the sweet spot. Most of the quality bass that I've seen pulled onto the sand with bucktails have been in schooling and blitz situations during the fall run when peanut bunker was the predominant bait. If the bass were on bigger baits, such as herring or adult bunker, I'd prefer a larger offering such as a pencil popper or metal-lipped swimming plug. If you find me on a sand beach while bass are pushing peanuts, I'll almost certainly be using a bucktail. In these situations, the larger bass tend to stay behind and under the main schools where they feed on falling scraps, and a bucktail is a great lure to get into their strike zone with a profile similar to the peanuts they're feeding on.

A TOOL WORTH MASTERING

This book is dedicated to the pursuit of trophy stripers. The "trophy" designation is somewhat subjective, but many think of it as referring to stripers over 40 pounds. From my own experiences, and having spent many years compiling surf fishing reports for Nor'east Saltwater, there is no doubt in my mind that the majority of surf-caught trophies fall to live eels, rigged eels, and bunker chunks. Despite this fact, there are situations in which big fish potential exists, but chunking and eeling are not good options. Facing into a raging Nor'easter, fishing deep moving water, or casting among a crowd in a specialized area such as under the Montauk Lighthouse are just a few examples where either conditions or etiquette make chunking and eeling inappropriate. It's in these settings where experienced bucktailers account for a significant portion of the trophy stripers that fall to artificials on our shores. While these skilled anglers can sometimes look like magicians as they hook fish after fish as nearby anglers struggle to hook up, they are doing nothing more than using the right combination of jig size, casting location, and retrieve style. With the determination to stick with the technique, and the discipline to pay attention to details, any angler can master what many consider the most productive lure on the striper coast.

CHAPTER THIRTEEN

ARTIFICIALS

By Bill Wetzel

Montauk Point, August 31st, 1997. All month long I was taking big stripers from the mid twenties to the low forties, with a consistent pick of mid thirty pound fish. After the new moon on August 3rd, things took off as the resident fish moved from the deep rips into the Montauk surf to feed on snappers. These young of the year bluefish were feasting on the loads of spearing that had recently come out from the shelter of the back bays. It sounded like a simple equation, find the snappers and in turn find the cows dining on the snappers. Yet hunting for big resident stripers is never an easy task and there is little comparison between hunting for the big girls and the schoolies. As usual, I had done my July daytime homework, searching for bait while walking the entire south side and driving from spot to spot on the north side of Montauk. The tides I fished were based on past patterns and related to wind and big heaves from offshore storms. Big Montauk resident August stripers will feed on very specific tides, as related to specific areas and conditions. To catch them you need to hone in on the patterns and fish very hard.

Rocky south side of Montauk, NY.

On this night I was working a double shift and was about 90 minutes from Montauk. My goal was to catch the last of the ebb tide beginning at 1:00 A.M. That required getting off of work at 10:00 P.M., making the drive to Montauk, gearing up and high tailing the mile walk deep on the south side into the "Land of the Giants." I would not recommend inexperienced surfcasters or anyone who does not know the terrain to fish these waters alone in the middle of the night. They are treacherous, especially if you have plans to rock hop, which of course I did.

It had been a quiet August, meaning very little big heaves, not much rain and consistent weather. These factors make for consistent fishing when the targets is August's resident cows. I remember the drive out there like it was yesterday. Very little wind and a clear dark night made my speedometer almost break though my dashboard. My hands clutched the wheel trembling with the big fish shakes. Ahhh yes, the big fish shakes! Ever had them? Upon my arrival, I geared up and made the mile walk over the dark, slippery boulders of Montauk's south side. Normally I fish eels during this month, but on that night I was fresh out of eels and had to revert to plugging. Under those conditions of flat water, no heave and snappers up the wazooo, the 7" black with gold tint Long A Magnum Bomber is my go-to plug.

I finally reached my destination right on time at 1:00 A.M. My plan was to wade out about 60 yards to a dreaded rock I affectionately call "death rock." The rock itself rises up about 3 feet from the ocean floor and has a small flat top, about 10 inches in diameter. If you do not already know where your rock is before you wade out, it will be very hard, if not impossible, to find a rock that you can stand on for long hours. While perched on "death rock", getting smacked around by waves, my toes hung over the front of the rock, heels over the rear, while my instep felt as if it was on a ball peen hammer. Oh yeah, I said it was a calm night, didn't I? It is until you wade about 60 yards into the ocean. However painful, "death rock" put me in a great position to fish a very specific piece of water, which I swear God himself put there just for me to target August cow stripers at low ebb.

I cannot tell you how many stars were out that night, but unfortunately I seemed to have plenty of time to gaze at them as my 7 inch Bomber had not been touched for over an hour. By about 2:30 A.M., I was getting nervous, as I had felt not so much as a touch. Suddenly out of nowhere, BAM, I get my first whack. I don't know what I was doing or thinking, but my concentration was not there and I missed the first fish. Cursing out loud, my mind eventually regained complete focus. It's the kind of focus that somehow blocks out everything else. The only thing in the world I am concentrating on is putting the plug in the right spot and retrieving it in a way that only a monster striper would love (at least, that is my hope). With no warning, my line took off, while the scream of my drag pierced the silence of the night. This was no 30 pound class fish! This was something special. With my rod bent in half, I remember praying that my 20 lb mono would not break. Yes, back then monofilament was all we used for line. As

I started to win the game of give and take, I saw her huge body roll about 20 feet in front of me. My initial thought was "My God, this is it. I may break the 50 pound mark." I finally got her near my perch and reached down and got my hand into the sweet spot under her gills. My entire body shook uncontrollably with excitement, as this was surely the biggest fish I had ever landed. Unfortunately, I did not have a scale. Therefore I could only estimate her weight as in the high forties. I could not live with

Bill Wetzel with an August cow.

myself if I told everyone that she was a 50 and I wasn't absolutely sure what she weighed. I know what you're thinking. Why didn't you keep her? A mile walk with a big fish was a hardship I was not interested in and killing a magnificent fish like that somehow just was not in my nature that night or, for that matter, most nights.

I mention this story because it is important to understand that the following discussion is about targeting large stripers only. I am hopeful that the above story illustrated the work, commitment and mindset it takes to target them and more importantly to find and actually land them.

It is impossible for me to use generalizations when discussing the how, when, where and why of finding and landing big stripers on plugs from the surf. It is imperative that you know the conditions and bait migrations in your specific area which have the best potential of producing trophies. It is vital that you understand that there is no secret plug or a secret color. The surfcaster must know the area he is fishing and put the correct plug in the correct water column, under the correct conditions. If he does this, he will reap the reward of catching big stripers! With the above said, I have chosen to focus most of this chapter using the Montauk surf as the example. However, I hope that after you have read this chapter, you will be able to relate similar strategies to your specific area.

The goal here is not necessarily to understand Montauk. It is more to help you understand my thinking (no matter how strange that may seem), as a surfcaster hunting for big stripers. Before getting into some specifics, it is important to have some knowledge of Montauk: "The Surfcasting Capital of the World". Due to its surrounding waters, rocky terrain and abundant structure, it is a natural stopover for many migrating game fish, including trophy striped bass. The Montauk Point lighthouse is located at the very eastern tip of Long Island. Running behind the lighthouse moving west are the areas referred to as the North side and the South side.

The North side is basically Block Island Sound and the South side is the Atlantic Ocean. I probably could write a one thousand page book on winds, tides and bait migrations, as related to time of year. However, for our purposes, we will focus on the prime times for trophy stripers as related to bait migration, time of year, current conditions and the plugs that will give you the best shot at a cow.

MINNOW TYPE SWIMMERS

I bet that if there were a poll taken among the hard-core surf rats, as to what plugs take trophy stripers; very few would say minnow type swimmers, such as Bombers or Red Fins. I am here to tell you that these plugs catch big fish under the right conditions. Let's break down the above August night into something I hope you can relate to. August is perhaps the toughest month to hunt for trophy stripers in the Montauk surf. The water temperatures are typically in the low to mid seventies and most of the fish are holding in deep cool water rips, outside of the surf zone. Forget about daytime bites, as it is just too hot, making August cow hunting a night game. The main advantage of fishing at this time of year is that it is pattern fishing for resident stripers at its finest. When I talk about resident pattern fishing, I mean fish that have been holding in an area for a long period of time and consistently feeding in a relatively confined area on specific tides. Toward the end of July or the beginning of August, usually around or on the first full or new moon, many of these fish come out of the deeper rips into the surf to feed. They feast on newly arrived snapper bluefish, which in turn are feeding on the vast schools of adult spearing that have recently made their way out of the back bays. The caster that puts in the time to find where the snappers and spearing are and notes the tides they appear, is the caster that will have the best shot at

Although most surfcasters don't consider minnow type swimmers "sexy", they are cow killers under the right conditions.

finding these August cows. Resident fish come from the deep rips into casting range to feed on August snappers usually after the first full or new August moon, whichever comes first. This by no means is based on any scientific studies. It is simply a theory of mine, based on years of observing what takes place in August in Montauk and taking notes on those observations. Many fishing theories you have to take with a grain of salt and I am sure that you have some theories of your own. That is just a part of the great game of surf fishing. Always ask yourself, does your theory hold true under real conditions? I know that this one does.

CONSIDERING TIDE

Now that we know the primary large bait is a snapper, let's explore why I picked the last two hours of the ebb tide to fish. Most casters would assume since it is August, the water temperatures are very warm and a flood tide would be best for large stripers. The reasoning behind this is that cooler water is flooding in from the ocean and larger stripers are more tolerant of cooler water temperatures. This is true in some cases and is a good assessment of the situation. In this case however, I had done my homework and found snappers feeding on spearing and determined that stripers were coming into the area to feed during the last two hours of the

Many things, including wind, tide and bait present, need to be taken into consideration when choosing which lure will be most effective.

ebb tide. The bottom of the tide also allowed me to wade out and cast into deeper water that was not accessible during high tide. These deeper water columns contained cooler water, which indeed is one of the factors an August cow hunter is looking for.

There are very few general assumptions when considering the best tides to target, no matter where you plan on fishing. Time of year, type of bait, water temperatures, moon and wind, will all play a role in what tide you choose to target trophy stripers. I recommend finding an area that "looks fishy", explore it and then fish that area at every tide stage. After assessing the structure, you may assume that the area is best fished at high ebb current during a SW wind, when in actuality, a NE wind combined with a low flood current produces a reachable rip on the edge of deep water. You can only gain that kind of information from actually fishing the structure. Areas that are shallow and have adjacent deep water are great areas to begin to hunt for cows. Bait will primarily hold in the shallows and big fish will either, move in and out of the shallows, using the deep water for cover or they may simply hold on the edge of the deep water, waiting for current to wash the bait into their strike zone. Whatever the case might be, do your homework to find the best tide/wind scenario for that particular area.

CONSIDER PRIMARY BAIT & WIND

In general, when fishing for large or small stripers, it is best to choose a plug that most closely matches the profile of the bait that is present in the water. You will also need to consider the water into which you are throwing the plug. Will the plug hold in the waves or will it get tossed about? Can you punch it through the wind? Does it dig deep enough or does it dig too deep? These are a few of the questions you should consider. On August 31st 1996, we had calm wind and not much white water. It is extremely difficult to throw a Bomber into a hard wind and nearly impossible to get it to hold in a water column in big water. On this night, since we had neither, I was provided with a couple of good reasons to throw it. However, the primary reason I selected the Bomber, is the profile of the plug. It is approximately the same length as most of the snappers that are present and the side profile is a close match as well. I should also let you know that these plugs work equally well during snapper bites in calmer back bay areas as well. On this night had I had a strong wind or big water, the Bomber would have been a poor choice, because I could not have punched it through the wind and it would not have held the big water. In other words, big water will toss these types of plugs about and you will not be able to maintain contact with the plug. The Long A Bomber has a dig of about one to three feet. You can really ride the plug on the very top of the water column with a very slow retrieve. Much of Montauk's south side is shallow, making a shallow running plug like the Long A Bomber a good choice. However, if you are fishing deep areas like jetties or inlets, a Bomber may not always be a good choice, as you may need to get down deep in the water column to where the large stripers are feeding.

COLOR CONSIDERATION

In this situation I used a black Bomber with gold tint. I know what you're thinking. Since when does a snapper have gold tint? Black and silver with a hint of lavender, olive or green maybe, but gold? I hear ya! It is just a confidence color that I have done well with in the past, especially when the primary bait are snappers. Another confidence color is black and silver. Color is rarely a big issue for me as a surfcaster. If you have confidence in the plug that you are throwing, you will in turn, have greater concentration and be more in tune to the conditions into which you are casting. My advice to you is to not get hung up on the color of your lure.

RETRIEVE CONSIDERATIONS

With the Bomber and similar minnow type plugs, I believe the retrieve is particularly important. Whether I am fishing for large or small stripers, I'll use a few different retrieves. After you have made your cast and have gained contact with the plug, the butt of the rod should be placed between your legs. Doing this will give you leverage when you set the hook and fight the fish. It will also (this is very important) give you better feel when you retrieve your plug. Your hand that is not reeling should be placed above the reel, with the backside of your knuckles on the rod itself. This hand should be open NOT closed, with the rod resting on the fingers. With the rod butt between your legs and the rod blank itself resting on your open fingers, you will be able to give the plug more action with superior feel. My usual initial retrieve is just a slow steady straight retrieve. You have no doubt heard of the saying, "If you think you are reeling too slow, you are reeling too fast." Well they ain't lying! Yet nothing in surf fishing is written in stone and on brighter nights, stripers are able to follow a faster moving target, therefore I have had great success speeding up my retrieve on brighter nights. This little tip however has not held true for slow moving, warm water, large August stripers. They almost always want it slow!

Nothing in surfcasting is written in stone. Experiment with your retrieve until you find the one that works.

Another go-to retrieve for me is a painfully slow retrieve with steady rod tip taps. This is a retrieve where the open fingers really come in handy. Here you just want to get the tip of the rod tapping ever so slightly. This is accomplished by short quick movements of the open fingers towards the body. This will cause your plug to flutter like a wounded baitfish on the surface. Try this same retrieve with a few quick intermittent cranks of the reel throughout the retrieve and you will have a few great retrieves to add to your arsenal. I usually like to make three casts with one retrieve, before moving on to the next. It is really important to make a mental note as to what retrieve the hit or fish came on. In the heat of the moment I will admit that there are many times I have forgotten what retrieve I was using and then had to start from the beginning. Putting a lot into the retrieve, as opposed to straight nothing retrieves, has been a topic of debate in the

"Surf Rats Ball" forums at www.longislandsurffishing.com on more than one occasion. Some call it throwing "junk" into the retrieves. I like to think of it as an art that can make a difference between catching or just getting wet.

EVERYWHERE AND ANYWHERE

From the 7" Long A magnum Bombers to Red Fins, Hellcats and Yo-Zuri minnow type swimmers, you can imitate an array of baitfish to catch trophy stripers from Cape Hatteras to Maine. In the above example I used a specific time in Montauk to imitate the primary bait, which were snappers. From Southern New Jersey to Rhode Island, the time for snappers is relatively the same: mid July through mid-September. During this period, the large minnow type swimmers are an excellent choice to throw to trophy stripers, as long as you know the specific conditions that will hold big stripers in your area. During these months surf temperatures are relatively warm. As mentioned, look for areas of shallow water (4-10 feet) adjacent to deep drop-offs (10 feet plus). Snappers and spearing will move in and out on the edges of drop-offs and lazy cows will lie in wait in the deeper cooler water to ambush incoming bait. If it is the big fish that you seek, I would recommend staying away from the back bays this time of year, as water temperatures there are just too warm and your chance at a true cow will almost certainly decrease. It is worth mentioning that in these back bay areas, especially from New York shores on up the striper coast, these months can be great for targeting smaller stripers using smaller size minnow type swimmers. Here, the primary baits are more than likely snappers and spearing. In general these smaller stripers feed on the spearing instead of the snappers, making the 3-½ inch or 4-½ inch Bombers a good choice.

SAND EELS

Another bait worth mentioning are sand eels. After having heated debates with many trophy striper seekers, I have found that most will tell you that a sand eel bite is not a trophy bite. Horse poo, I say! Sand eels are found throughout the striper coast and can produce a fantastic bite of large fish. I will freely admit that I have never taken a striper over 30 pounds on strictly a sand eel bite, but I have caught many in the mid twenty to upper twenty pound range, when stripers were strictly on sand eels. The 4.5" chicken scratch Bomber is one of my premier choice plugs for this type of bite. The 7" yellow Hellcats have a thinner profile and are even a better choice, however the Hellcats are no longer made and are tougher every year to keep in stock. The color of a chicken scratch Bomber is basically yellow and does not really match the color of sand eels. Not to mention that the profile of the Bomber is far from the profile of a sand eel. Then why does this combo work so well? I have no idea, but I do know that indeed it is a killer. What about the trophies? Yes, there are trophy fish to be had during a sand eel bite. The key is knowing that large bait such as shad or herring are feeding on the sand eels. In Montauk for example, it is known among the locals and regulars, that the sand eels show up on a particular 5-mile stretch of sand beach, during the first two weeks of July or thereabouts. Hold-over herring and shad are devouring these sand eels. Guess what is feeding on the herring and shad? Yep, monster stripers.

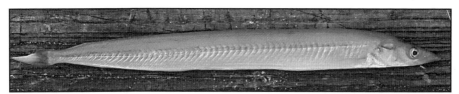

When sand eels are on the striper's menu, stick with long, narrow type lures. Many memorable nights occurred over the years when large sand eels populated the surf.

THE DARTER

It is May 5th, a few days after the new moon, with water temps at about 49 degrees. It is a mostly cloudy cool day, with air temperatures in the low fifties. High tide was at 8 PM and you have chosen to fish the first two hours of the flood current from 2:30 A.M. - 4:30 A.M. This is a tide that allows you to wade to some outer rocks and fish a very productive water column on the North side of Montauk. Higher tides would put you into more shallow water columns that are much closer to the beach and less productive. The night air is brisk with no wind, as the moisture from your breath rises slowly to the heavens above. You expect that on the night tides, the adult bunker mixed in with shad have been coming up on the

Jones Reef, located on the north side of Montauk Point, N.Y.

flatter areas to feed on krill, as this has been the pattern year after year since you can remember. Your decision for this approach is based on past patterns and your hope is that Mrs. Cow will also be up on these flats, feeding on these large baits.

As a cow hunter who uses plugs as his primary weapon, there are some plug questions that you should be asking yourself. What is the best plug for this situation and why? What size should the plug be and why? What color should be used and why? What would be the best retrieve for this situation? Now for the tough part, choosing a plug. Fear not! A darter fits the bill perfectly. The darter presents a large profile, with a zig-zag action that horizontally covers a good amount of the water you are targeting. The amount of water a darter covers is seldom talked about but it's very significant. Compare the water coverage of a darter to most other plugs; minnow type swimmers, needlefish, bottle plugs, poppers etc. None have a zigzag motion that covers the water as much as a darter. In general, darters work best in current as their design enables them to dig down into a current, creating their own action. During the first two hours of a flood current, on the north side of Montauk, while wading out to the outer rocks, you'll have plenty of current to work the darter.

TIDE, WINDS AND WATER TEMPERATURES

It is interesting to note that it is early May and I have targeted a flood tide instead of an ebb tide. During this time of year water temperatures range from about 47-51 degrees in the Montauk surf. Early spring areas near inlets or bays will have warmer water on ebb flow on sunny days, because they are shallower and will heat up more quickly than open waters. This is common knowledge among back bay fishermen, who target ebbing water at the mouth of marsh drains at dusk. For those of you that do not know what a drain is, it is simply an area where a smaller body of water drains into a larger body of water. Drains are found in marshes throughout the striper coast. Back bay fishermen know that a sunny day will warm the low tide mud bottoms of these shallow marshy areas. In turn, the water will warm as it floods the area and become especially warm as it drains on ebb tide. The water temperature may be as much as 10 degrees warmer in these areas. Knowing that the north side of Montauk is the Block Island Sound and has many estuaries dumping into it on an ebb tide, why was the flood chosen? In the above scenario it was a cloudy, cold day. Although Montauk's North side has potentially warmer water draining into it, the water coming out of the estuaries on this day is going to be cooler than the water coming in from the ocean, due to the

This cow fell to a Super Strike darter, worked over Montauk's south side rocks.

overcast cold day. Water temperatures may only vary a degree or two, but that is sometimes enough to spark a bite or to put a bite down.

RETRIEVE CONSIDERATIONS

In early spring low water temperature, big bass are not going to chase a fast moving target or fight big water, no matter where you are fishing. In the above situation you have a very quiet night, which is perfect for this time of year. These fish are lying up on the reef or flats, nosing into the current, utilizing whatever holes, rocks or available structure there is to ambush larger baits. In this case, a slow retrieve is essential because the water temps are cold and the big ones are not going to chase fast moving targets. Whenever plugging, maintaining contact is extremely important. If your line is slack and there is no contact, speed up the retrieve until contact is regained. No contact = No fish! I would recommend not buying into the idea that darters have to be fished slowly or are strictly for areas with good current. You can speed up the retrieve during bright nights, under bridges or in areas where there is light. They are also very effective in the daylight when using faster retrieves. Stripers make their approach to a plug by sight and on brighter nights or during daylight hours, faster retrieve speeds can provoke strikes more than slower speeds. On a quiet night, I like to give a slight twitch of the rod tip with every 4 or 5 turns of the reel. The twitch will create a little extra zig for the zag. As with the Bomber, use an open hand to get the best feel for the movement of the plug. On windy nights with stronger current, I will usually just use a straight slow retrieve, as the feel for the plug becomes minimal, therefore trying to twitch the tip of the rod becomes useless. In areas with little or no current, I like to use short hard twitches to get the plug to dart. This is a great little trick when big baits are present in quieter waters.

COLOR

As already stated, I was never big on color for most situations in the suds. Heck, that is not a true statement. There was a time when I was very big on color and used to waste time changing colors only to find that most of the time it made no difference. Now I have a little more salt in my veins and believe that you have to put the right profile plug into the right water column with the right retrieves. If stripers are there with the feedbag on, they will pounce on your plug, regardless of color. On the other hand, I have been in situations on the darkest of nights when only one color would produce. However these situations are very rare. With this in mind, I have to go with the color yellow for the situation presented. For the most part, the North side of Montauk is fairly bright, if not from the lighthouse, then from the town lights as you move further west. This is perhaps the reason why yellow has taken more trophy stripers than any other color in Montauk. Hmmm, or perhaps it is because more casters use yellow than any other color. Heck, I don't really know, just throw yellow in the above situation! Only the fish really know. I kind of go with the saying, on a dark night use a dark plug. Many will tell you that a darker plug's profile can be seen more easily than a lighter plug's profile on a dark night. I don't know! I am not a fish and most of the literature on this matter is confusing. I have used white darters on dark nights and blurple on bright nights and done well on both. I have always had great confidence in the yellow but gold has often been deadly. Any plug with a little or a lot of gold in it seems to work extremely well, especially for larger fish. If you find that porgies or juvenile weakfish are in the surf zone, it is an especially good time to get out the gold. The problem is finding plug makers that make gold plugs. I have a theory behind this as well. Gold is not a good color

A gold darter is one of Bill Wetzel's favorite lures, especially when juvenile weakfish are in the surf zone.

for the plug collectors, however it is a great color for the fishermen. Are there more plug collectors than fishermen these days? Maybe…

BAIT

The darter is a plug that effectively fits the profile of most bait throughout the striper coast. What big baits do you have in your area? Bunker, shad, snappers, juvenile weakfish, squid, porgies, mullet, the list goes on and on. In the case above, a 2 3/8oz Super Strike darter will more than likely get the job done, as it darts and zig-zags its way over prime real estate. For a larger profile darter, with a deeper swim, try a Gibbs 3 oz darter. These plugs have a serious dig and will get you down to where the fish are. However, due to the smaller surface area, a 2 3/8-ounce Super Strike will outcast a 3-ounce Gibbs. Just as a 2 ounce Gibbs bottle plug will outcast a 3-ounce Gibbs bottle plug, but the 3-ounce version will dig harder and faster.

THE MAKER

These days there are a zillion plug builders out there, with everything from custom plugs that catch anglers more than fish, to very expensive wood that will catch fish and break your wallet at the same time. I have to be honest here and tell you that I throw 2 3/8 ounce Super Strike darters 99% of the time. In the above situation, that is what I am throwing. They were designed by perhaps the most influential plug builder of our time, Don Musso. It is rare that you will hear casters talk about consistency in a plug, but consistency is one of the main reasons I choose Super Strike over other brands. By consistency, I mean when you throw the plug in the middle of the night, you can trust that it will swim exactly like all the other super strike darters, 100% of the time. It is astonishing to me that darters are not a go-to big fish plug in many areas of the striper coast. Well known striper nut Dr. Charlie Ruger fishes up and down the coast throughout the season. One of the areas he hits every year is Oregon inlet in Cape Hatteras. "We always fished at night so the locals never caught on. They just started to catch on to what we were doing (throwing darters) a few years ago. They called them banana plugs. Now more guys are doing it, but darters are still pretty much non-existent there." C'mon

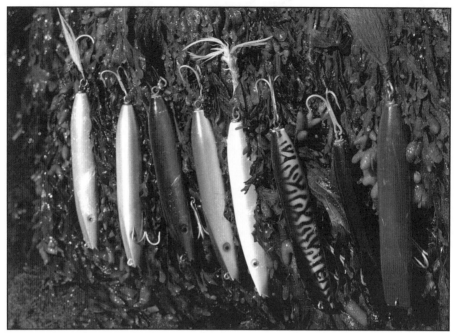

Darters have accounted for more cows landed on Montauk's rocky shores than any other lure.

everybody, wake up to one of the best big fish catching plugs available (under the right conditions)!

THE PENCIL POPPER

I hate this plug! To see a zillion guys lined up on a beach with a 10 or 11-foot rod stuck between their legs, violently shaking it back and forth, is an ungodly sight. Perhaps the pencil popper is used most by New Jersey rats fishing the fall run in Montauk, New Jersey rats fishing Nantucket, New Jersey rats fishing Cape Cod, New Jersey rats hitting New Jersey on the huge bunker schools, or heck I'll just admit that this plug is "New Jersey's Death Machine." Sometimes I will see a bunch of guys from the Garden State lined up on the south side of Montauk, catching fish on this damn plug and I will be forced to throw something else, just to show the world that stripers can be caught on something besides a pencil popper. For as much venom as I have for these plugs I am forced to use them, because they are trophy plugs, as New Jersey surf rat "Foul Mouth" Bob pointed out to me one August morning.

About 10 years ago I convinced Bob of the great August fishing in Montauk. Foul Mouth Bob McCloskey stands about 5 foot something, with a hunched back, dark graying hair and teeth that he only puts in when he has to chew something he really likes. He has been at this game for a long time and has a great understanding of striper movements, which he will be happy to explain to you, as long as you can handle a few well-placed adjectives. One August night we had 7 to 9 foot rollers coming into the Montauk south side surf. I was in my buggy sound asleep in the lower parking lot of Montauk Point, when the striper alarm went off at 2 A.M. I pounded on Bob's van door and screamed " Wake up, the tide waits for no man". I heard the pleasant reply, "#$@% yoouuuu" which only meant Bob was ready to go. We made the long walk through the night, deep on the south side of Montauk. Huge water was hitting the beach and I was thankful to have a buddy with me. It can be a scary place 60 yards out into the ocean standing on a rock in the middle of the night with waves coming in that block out the horizon. We made our way out to our rocks and fished through the night for not a touch. At first light the bite began. We started banging one schoolie after another on bucktails. After about 20 minutes of this Bob screamed through the roar of the pounding surf, "#$@% this, I'm putting on a pencil popper." "The water is too big," I

A 3 ounce Lex pencil popper worked side to side fooled this large striper.

screamed back. My thinking was that the plug was just going to get tossed around too much in the big water. He would never be able to maintain contact with the plug long enough to catch anything. Sure enough, on Bob's first cast he was leaning into a fish, screaming some gibberish over the mayhem. When the water is big, it is extremely oxygenated and the stripers are completely jacked up. You want a fight? Go catch stripers in big water. This bass was a fat mid-teen bass, as Bob bragged as much as he could over the roar about how the pencil popper only catches big fish. "Big deal, a teen schoolie," I thought to myself. Then it was another teen fish and then a few twenty plus fish, as I continued to stand my ground throwing bucktails, still only catching schoolies. As I was contemplating burying my pride and making the switch to the pencil, I saw Bob leaning into a fish that had large written all over it. About 10 minutes later, Bob was reaching down in the suds holding up a very nice fish. We later weighed it at 35 lbs and to this day I have never heard the end of how effective pencil poppers are for big fish. Yeah, yeah, yeah!

BAIT IMITATION

Trying to figure out why pencil poppers are so effective or what bait they imitate, is like trying to figure out how the earth was formed. Just accept that you're not going to figure this out. I have heard that it is a great snapper imitation, bunker imitation, even a sand eel imitation, yet to this day I have never seen any baitfish act like a pencil popper. Therefore, I am going to offer you my theory. "A pencil popper does not imitate anything." When a striper hits a pencil popper, it is one of the most violent strikes you will ever see. This is one of the reasons I believe that the strike comes out of pure aggression. Think about this: a school of stripers have worked a pod of anchovies for the past 20 minutes. They have finally managed to push the anchovies into a cove after working over a quarter mile stretch of beach. Along comes Mr. Pencil Popper, slashing back and forth disrupting the anchovies. The anchovies disperse and the pencil popper gets attacked. Attacked out of aggression or bait imitation? How about large stripers holding to a structure? Consider this. A small group of 30 pound + stripers are holding to a specific piece of structure, waiting for a meal to pass by, therefore using the least amount of energy possible. Along comes the pencil popper disrupting their feed and they smack it with a vengeance. Whatever the reason, this plug can be used whenever any bait is present as it is a "non-specific bait" plug.

DAY VERSUS NIGHT

Unlike the bomber and darter, the pencil popper is primarily a daytime plug. Most trophy stripers will come into the surf during the hours of darkness, but daytime has its place for big fish. During the past five or so years from late May to early July, most of the New Jersey coast has seen some of the best trophy striper fishing in history. The reason? Bunker! Massive schools of bunker have returned and cow stripers are on their heels. This bite can happen at dawn, dusk or in the middle of the day, but it is the pencil popper that out-catches any other plug. In other parts of the striper coast, dawn and dusk, combined with a good tide and the right conditions, can be phenomenal with the pencil popper. The right conditions, meaning you may not want to throw this plug to an area that has 60' of water unless you know that the fish are feeding on or near the surface, as this is a surface plug. Instead look for shallow water areas that are adjacent to deep water.

Yes, the pencil popper can be used in the dark, but it is far more effective in the light. Stripers are going to have a tough time following this target in the dark, however if worked slower, with fewer splashes, it can be extremely effective. Many casters will not work the plug at all during the night. Instead, just a slow retrieve with no rod tip action can be effective. I have heard of good catches using it as it was meant to be used (with a slashing back and forth motion) in the dark, but for me personally this has never been effective. For me, there are so many more effective plugs for a night bite that the pencil rarely sees the inside of my night plug bag for night bites. Then again, conditions, conditions, conditions!

TECHNIQUE

Hands down, the pencil popper is the hardest plug to work properly. I fish with a gentleman who has been in the suds since I was in diapers. "I don't know what it is? I just can't get my left hand to go slow, while at the same time moving the other one fast" is what I hear from him every time we get into a pencil bite. It is a technique that I usually cannot teach my customers in one outing. The following is the pencil popper technique I teach to my customers.

Make your cast. After the plug hits the water, make contact with the plug as quickly as possible. After contact is made, lock the butt of the rod between your legs, by squeezing your legs together. This is a key component. You should not be able to pull the rod out from between your legs once the rod is locked. Begin to retrieve just fast enough to maintain contact with the plug, no faster. Place your hand that is not reeling just below the first guide on the rod. Grip the rod so that your thumb is braced against the backside side of the rod. Doing this will significantly assist you in working and guiding the rod. While keeping the retrieve speed slow, move the rod tip violently back and forth. The key here is to focus on the rod tip by getting it to move back and forth, not side to side or a circular motion, as this will not give the plug the proper action. If the butt of the rod is shaking while you are trying to get this action, it means that you have the entire rod moving instead of the just the tip. The butt should always remain quiet; therefore make sure it is locked between your legs. If you are working the pencil properly, it should have a side-to-side, walk the dog motion while moving through the water at a slow pace. Water will spray from left to right at each whip of the tip.

Many times stripers will miss the plug completely. If this happens there are two schools of thought. Many surfcasters will stop the plug for a couple of seconds and the stripers will either hit the plug during the stop or at the start of the retrieve. Ninety- nine percent of the time I personally use a continuous retrieve no matter what, which means never stopping. I have also found that if a striper actually touches the plug, but the hook set is missed, that striper will almost never come back at the plug if you stop the retrieve.

COLOR

I really believe that in the case of the pencil popper being fished for big fish, it is extremely rare that color plays a role. Perhaps in the back bays where there is gin clear water, a case can be made for different colors. There are those that will argue this point so you will have to use colors that

When working pencil poppers, grip the rod so that your thumb is braced against the backside of the rod.

you develop confidence in. Generally, I use white pencil poppers, but I have tried yellow, mackerel, silver, blue, yellow and who knows what other colors and have experienced little difference. There are always exceptions, so be prepared with some different colors just in case. One exception that I can recall was a time when we had a good bite of large stripers that were on squid. A pink pencil popper was out fishing any other color ten to one.

TYPE

There are basically two types of pencil poppers. All have a thin profile in the front of the plug with a gradual flare outward to the rear. They are weighted in the rear, which makes the rear of the plug sink below the surface and the front of the plug float above the surface. One type is the common pencil popper made with a round belly and the other type has a flat belly towards the front of the plug. The flat-bellied pencil popper is usually the one I use when fishing big water and targeting large stripers. Its profile enables the plug to cut through wind more efficiently and it will also hold big water slightly better than its sibling. Two of my favorite flat-bellied pencils are the 3-ounce Gibbs Canal Special and the 3-ounce Lex. These plugs will fly like rockets and handle almost any big water condition that Mother Nature throws at you.

Few things are more exciting, then watching a big bass attack a pencil popper.

PLUG TWEAKS

I am completely against using snaps, to change plugs. Yes it is a quick change, but snaps can open. I always hear the argument "I have only had one snap open" or "It has only happened to me a few times." Do you really want to take that chance when you have put all this time, effort and money into catching a trophy striper? Well I don't! My advice is to take the extra 15-30 seconds to tie direct. It will pay off in the end. For most plugs that swim: minnow type swimmers, darters, bottle plugs, etc., I will use a split ring attached to the eye of the plug. Then tie directly to the split ring. This will allow the plug to move freely and give it its natural movement. Be sure not to tie your knot at the split ring gap, as this may cut your line. I cannot emphasize enough to purchase quality split rings. As of this writing I only use Spro stainless split rings. I often get asked " What about a loop knot"? I do not use loop knots because, although they will enable the plug to move freely, the loop will be compromised as it slides back and forth through the eye of the plug. This creates friction and all too often the leader will break at this point in the loop.

It is extremely important to have quality hooks. As of this writing many plug manufacturers may make a great plug, but in many cases the hooks they put on them are inferior. One of the reasons for this is that some hook

Conditions have a big influence on which lures will be most productive on any given day.

companies have compromised their quality and now are making garbage hooks that will not withstand even small fish. These inferior hooks are made with open eyes, which make it easy for a plug manufacturer to put on the plug. Other superior hooks like VMC hooks are only made with closed eyes, making one more step for the manufacturers to get the hook onto the plug. I would recommend that if you do not know the make of the hooks on the plugs, call or write the manufacturer to find out. If they are not VMC hooks, more than likely they are inferior and you will need to change them. Many surf rats use split rings to attach the closed eye hooks to the plug. The argument is that it allows the hook to hang lower thereby perhaps decreasing a striper's chance of getting leverage on the hook and spitting out the plug. Personally, I cut the eye of a closed eye hook with a small pair of bolt cutters. Then I use pliers to open the eye of the hook and attach it directly to the hanging barrel swivel of the plug. At this time I am trying to determine if I have dropped more fish using this method as opposed to the split ring method. Hmmm?

You should know that when targeting big stripers, most plugs come with hooks that are too small in my opinion. The Super Strike darter for example, comes with 3/0 hooks. I will cut the 3/0 hooks off and replace them with 4/0's. This gives a big fish less chance of getting leverage on the hooks and crushing them. Yes, when you are fishing for large stripers, they will sometimes annihilate the hooks on your plug.

My overall recommendation is to keep things as simple as possible. Do not put too many terminal tweaks on a plug. Tie direct. Keep color schemes simple. The more terminal tackle you add, the more of a chance that something will go wrong.

OTHER PLUGS

The three plugs addressed in this chapter are by no means the only plugs you should be using to target trophy stripers. Needle fish, bottle plugs, hellcats, spooks, little neck poppers, metal lip swimmers, tins, etc. all have their place given a particular condition. Learn how to use all of them under a variety of conditions and you will take your share of big fish.